THE EDUCATION

OF AUGIE MERASTY

NEW EDITION

THE EDUCATION
OF AUGIE MERASTY

a residential school memoir

JOSEPH AUGUSTE MERASTY

with David Carpenter

Printed and bound in Canada at Marquis.

Library and Archives Canada Cataloguing in Publication

Merasty, Joseph Auguste, author
The education of Augie Merasty : a residential school memoir /
Joseph Auguste Merasty with David Carpenter. — New edition.
(The Regina collection)

Issued in print and electronic formats.
ISBN 978-0-88977-457-5 (hardcover).—ISBN 978-0-88977-468-1 (PDF).—
ISBN 978-0-88977-469-8 (HTML)

1. Merasty, Joseph Auguste—Childhood and youth. 2. Cree Indians—
Biography. 3. Native students—Canada—Biography. 4. Indians of North
America—Canada—Residential schools. 5. Cree Indians—Education—Canada.
I. Carpenter, David, 1941-, author II. Title. III. Title: Augie Merasty.
IV. Series: Regina collection

E96.5.M47 2017   371.829'97071   C2016-907620-2   C2016-907621-0

University of Regina Press
Saskatchewan, Canada, s4s 0A2
TEL: (306) 585-4758 FAX: (306) 585-4699
web: www.uofrpress.ca

10 9 8 7 6 5 4 3 2 1

We acknowledge the support of the Canada Council for the Arts for
our publishing program. We acknowledge the financial support of the
Government of Canada. / Nous reconnaissons l'appui financier du
gouvernement du Canada. This publication was made possible through
Creative Saskatchewan's Creative Industries Production Grant Program.

 Canada Council Conseil des Arts   Canadä   creative
for the Arts   du Canada   SASKATCHEWAN

Contents

A Note on the Text—vii
Augie and Me: An Introduction,
*   by David Carpenter*—ix
Map: Sturgeon Landing and other places
*   discussed in this book*—xxxviii

ONE   School Days, School Days—1
TWO   Hard Times—11
THREE   The Passion of Sister Felicity—17
FOUR   The Loves of Languir and Cameron—23
FIVE   Brotherly Love and the Fatherland—29
SIX   Father Lazzardo among the Children—37
SEVEN   Sisters of the Night—41
EIGHT   Lepeigne—45
NINE   Revenge—51
          Conclusion—59

Afterword by David Carpenter—65
Postscript by David Carpenter—75
Study Guide—81
Acknowledgements—95

A Note on the Text

THIS IS A BOOK OF NONFICTION, AN ATTEMPT BY a man and his editor to expose an injustice that happened more than seven decades ago. I have changed some of the names of people and places in Augie's account to protect the identities of individuals and their families. I have not changed the name of Joseph Auguste Merasty. The names of our country's heroes and martyrs should be proclaimed. —D.C.

Augie and Me:

AN INTRODUCTION

IN THE SPRING OF 2001, I RECEIVED A PHONE CALL
from the Department of English at the University of Saskatchewan, where I had been a professor before becoming
a full-time writer. One of the women in the office had
received a letter, addressed to the "dean of the University
of Saskatchewan," from an old fellow up north requesting
some help with his memoir. The man was a retired Cree
trapper in his early seventies who lived in the bush. He
wanted a co-writer to come up to his cabin, tape his stories, and write them down for publication. Particularly,
he asked the dean to recommend someone who had "a
good command of the English language," someone who
might also have an outdoorish streak. Were this scribe
to agree to help him write his book, he would "enjoy

the finest fishing in all of Saskatchewan." The man was building his cabin "right at the junction of two beautiful rivers that join together."

Luckily, the letter found its way to the English department. "Dear Sir," it began, "I really don't know where to begin or how to ask someone of your high position this rather odd request, and coming from a retired fisherman and trapper and Jack of all trades I might add." The man had already finished writing down his stories of the horrors that he and his schoolmates had been subjected to "at that terrible place" known as St. Therese Residential School in the community of Sturgeon Landing. I had never heard of the school, which he described as "about forty miles south of Flin Flon" and about "the same distance north of The Pas." These two coordinates are at the western edge of northern Manitoba, near the Saskatchewan border, but the school and the community of Sturgeon Landing are on the other side of the border, in Saskatchewan. Back in the early 1970s, a year or two before I got my job as an English professor, I completed a weekend workshop in The Pas, and memories of time spent in that community still trouble me. When I was there, The Pas was a town divided hatefully between white and Native peoples.

The old trapper correspondent described his "superiors" at the residential school, the priests, brothers and nuns, as primarily "white" and "French Canadian." The stories he had written down and sent off were for "the law group representing us across Canada." He was referring to the Working Group on Truth and Reconciliation and of the Exploratory Dialogues (1998–1999), which constituted the first stage of the Truth and Reconciliation Commission. The working group sought written testimonies from former victims of the residential school system, which came into being in Canada around 1870 and lasted for more than a century in many parts of the country. Joseph Auguste (Augie) Merasty attended St. Therese Residential School from 1935 to 1944 at a time when there was "no law" up there to prevent the many atrocities committed by the children's "superiors."

Merasty had already written his story down for the purposes of the inquiry. So, at the time, I wondered why he needed someone to drive way up north to tape them. I suspected then, as I do now, that the legal firm representing Merasty had some hesitation about releasing his account while it was still before the inquiry and on its way to the courts.

"Sorry," Merasty continued in his letter, "I am getting carried away here, I will state my reasons for asking the request to you, Mr. Professor, and Dean of University. I want to very humbly ask you sir to ask someone in your class, someone who has a good command of the English language, to help me write a book I fully intend to write beginning about the first week in August 2001." First, Merasty suggested that he had to finish work on his cabin and tie up a few loose ends. The cabin was to be finished by the end of June 2001. He wanted his co-writer to stay for two weeks in the cabin while recording his stories. They could discuss the payment later. They would talk and they would fish for "northern pike up to twenty-five pounds, [for] whites and pickerel, and many more."

He concluded, "We be having a great time for sure."

Merasty made the point in this first of many letters that he would not only tell his story but also those of many others. He would tell of things that happened from 1927, "eight years before [he] entered." His "older sisters, aunties, uncles and others told [him] things that happened in their time." He came to believe their stories because "the same things happened in the time [he] was there." By telling the stories of others and connecting them to his own experiences, Merasty broadened his range of inquiry, and in other, subtler ways, he broadened the implications of his sometimes horrific story, a story in which our entire nation is darkly and obscurely complicit.

❈ ❈ ❈

WRITERS, LIKE OTHER professionals, can get very busy. If they are to make their deadlines and finish their books so that they can get paid for their work, they learn to say no to a lot of people. They become willing slaves to their own prioritized, underpaid, preoccupied, inward-dwelling lives. It was in that writerly state that I, at first, said no to Augie—as I soon came to know him—and his scheme to bring me, my spinning rod, and my tape recorder to the North. On the phone, I asked him to send me a copy of the story he had written for the commission, and he said he could not get copies of his submission.

Suddenly, I began to realize something of the challenge that faced Augie, living in a cabin in the bush without electricity and sometimes without a car, far from any town, on a new reserve with only three other houses. My question to Augie, "Why didn't you get photocopies of your submission?" seemed somehow beside the point.

Until this moment on the phone, Augie was irrepressible, all enthusiasm, the voice of endless possibilities.

"Augie," I said, "I need you to write this story down. All of it. Before I can come and help you."

Silence.

"If I'm going to help you write your memoir, I need something more than a bunch of tapes to transcribe."

Silence.

"What if I phoned your lawyers and asked for copies of your story? Do you think that would help?"

Silence, and then a weary voice muttering from some

outpost five hundred kilometres north of Saskatoon, "Ohhh, David, I dunno. I think maybe I gotta try a few things, ah?"

Soon after our conversation, Augie sent me a copy of a note he had recently written to the lawyers who represented him in the Truth and Reconciliation Commission inquiries:

> I am in the process of making the whole story from the time I entered St. Therese from 1935 to 1944 when I left. It is a book I hope to finish within the next couple of months, with some help from English Professor David Carpenter, who had written eight books and also had them published. Him and I communicate at times by phone or letter, and he wants me to do what I can to complete the book. I've done about one hundred and fifty pages already and have about two hundred pages to go, and I've sent him some manuscripts and I will send him everything whenever I am finished, sometime before Easter.

> Joseph A. Merasty

I frequently heard about the 150 pages done and the two hundred pages to go, but for reasons that I will try to outline, in the eight years of our correspondence following this letter, I never saw all the pages that Augie referred to and promised to send me.

I heard little from Augie throughout the spring, summer, and fall of 2001, but in late November he wrote me a letter in a downcast mood. Instead of working on his memoir or finishing his cabin, Augie had been travelling and drinking a lot.

> I fell off the wagon after my lady friend of ten years decided that [I] should not see her. . . . We have lived together in ten different apartments and houses and I was happy and always assumed I was going to ride into the sunset with her. I have never loved or cared for anyone . . . like her in the last forty-five years. . . . It's a long story so I won't delve on it. I got her the job at the Casino by filling out her resume, I also showed her how to drive a car. All of these she's never found time or inclination to obtain in the past. She was too busy drinking and running around. She has . . . shacked up with nine different men and had nine bastards from each one of them. I now wonder why I was so crazy about her all these years, no matter what she did to me, stealing money when I

passed out, bringing other guys [to] her place whenever she wanted to.

The story continued in great detail with old cars traded in for new ones at Augie's expense, and old Augie being traded in for a younger model, as well. He was thirty years older than this girlfriend, and in the end, she found someone her own age. Readers will no doubt recognize the universality of Augie's romantic woes. This is not simply the story of a Cree man being ditched by a Cree woman in Prince Albert. It's a story as old and as sad as the blues.

We exchanged one or two letters during the winter, and Augie's missives turned into long lists of loss from long bouts of boozing, and his tone remained glum. Then in late February of 2002, almost three months after his first gloomy letter, Augie struck a different note. "At the end of your last letter I found it rather amusing [that you] find the time to mention Aubergine [the con woman who jilted Augie], and you are absolutely right." I had told Augie that he was probably lucky to have escaped her clutches.

"I almost went 'BATS,'" Augie continued, "but I now realize what a fool I really was." He cited a number of similar cases of heartbreakers and con women from the tabloids he read, and he heartily identified with their victims. In the same letter, Augie went on to recall the first terrible heartbreak of his life. "I once contemplated ending it all twenty-three years ago when my wife of thirty years left me. It took approximately five years to get back down to earth. I feel lucky I came out alive from the cesspool of booze. This time it only took months and I been dry for some time now."

What resilience, I remember musing. I thought we had lost Augie to despair and worse, and here he was at age seventy-two, ready to start again. From his earliest days at St. Therese he demonstrated this resilience in the face of terrifying and degrading attacks. When I began to connect the resilient, oppressed child with the alcoholic, love spurned old man, my feelings for Augie began to climb up the moral ladder from abhorrence to pity to sympathy to empathy. I just had to meet this guy face to face.

By the end of the winter of 2002, I was receiving regular mailings of his residential school story. One letter contained the photocopy of some twenty-seven pages (slightly more than eight thousand words) of Augie's sprawling but immaculate handwriting. Another letter contained thirteen pages of foolscap (about five thousand words). The other enclosures were shorter, most of them originals but some photocopied. I could not tell if his lawyers had released these disorganized swatches of handwriting or if Augie had written them for my benefit and done the photocopying himself. Sometimes I would end up with several retellings of a gruelling episode I had transcribed earlier, so I would incorporate the best of each version into one version to get the clearest picture of the incident. I discovered that there was a wide gulf between the Augie at the end of his rope, singing the blues, and Augie the truth-seeking memoirist who recounted his experiences with painful clarity. In one version, one of his assailants was a "perverted so and so." In another, more clearly rendered version of the same story, he was "an emeritus of immorality."

The stories assembled in this volume make for a compelling but rambling account for readers, people like you and me—willing witnesses to the ongoing tragedy of Native peoples who suffered from their collision with Euro-white justice, domination, and broken promises. Augie talks at length about the dreaded Brother Lepeigne and then moves on to some other atrocity, some other adventure, then returns to Brother Lepeigne with yet another brutal encounter, as though his former keeper still haunts his every day. Augie's letters were even more pronounced examples of this cyclical tendency, especially if he had been drinking or felt gloomy.

Augie's reports of being sexually assaulted twice by his nemesis, "Brer" Lepeigne, were very detailed but at times confused. I did my best to assemble only one attack and describe it in Augie's terms, as graphically as he did. Augie seemed to think that Lepeigne's attacks on several other boys "gave" them homosexuality in adult life. Like many people of his generation, Augie seems confused between the terms "homosexual" and "pedophile." Lepeigne comes across as the latter, but the possibility of his homosexuality is not really explored in Augie's account.

In my conversations with Augie and in my editing of his accounts, I tried not to correct him. I tried, instead, to nudge him and his stories into clarity. "It is fifty-seven years since I left that school," he told me, "and I find it hard to remember all that has happened to me and others." The final product in this account, then, is a collaboration between a man haunted by memories and an editor bombarding him with questions and goading him toward the milestones and the foundations of his own memory.

Late in 2003 I received a long letter from Augie that recapped the sorrows of his life: his habit of driving all over the North and the western provinces to fight off despair, the long drinking bouts he had resumed, and the many deaths in his extended family that saddened him so.

In the midst of his grieving, Augie had arrived at a point where he could begin to cherish what was left of his people. "I am coming along real well with my own family and all their kids, I am really enjoying myself in all things I do for the first time in a long time. I really feel I'm walking in the light. I feel as though I can take whatever this old world can dish out. Oh! I know I've tried [to quit drinking] dozens of times, but now at my age, I know, I have limited time, and that's no Bull."

Augie confessed that, over the past three years (2000 to 2003), he had lost "hundreds of pages" of his memoir to theft, to periods of extended drinking, to sheer care-lessness. "I don't want to sound like a bigot," he told me, "but ninety-five per cent of my people are drunks and thieves and they take anything they can find. I have been a victim of such individuals all my life. I never seem to learn, always too dumb or too trusting."

Note how Augie lapsed in tone from the euphoria and resolve of a man on the mend to the self-pity of a man who has fallen. Augie issued these laments when the booze had taken him into a dark place; at other times, he was no doubt aware that the 95 per cent he referred to were merely the drunkest of his brethren and hardly representative of all northern First Nations people. He ended that letter with a promise: "As of now I am one hundred per cent sure that I am going to finish what I have started. And for many reasons of my own, and for others who are beholden to me, I swear I will." Those words were penned eleven years ago, but I received very little of his memoir after that.

I don't know how much I need to despair over the scattered and lost pages of his life. Perhaps they will show up in scraps here and there, or, more likely, they are gone for good. I suppose that I am simply grateful for the stories he did send me. His memoir rests on these 75 handwritten pages, as well as on the letters he sent me.

In one of his letters from that up-and-down time of his life, dated September 18, 2003, Augie reported that he was at last finishing his cabin, doing some adjustments on the door and windows. His cabin is on the Peter Ballantyne Cree Nation Reserve at Birch Portage, just off the Hanson Lake Road, west of Creighton. He was about to go moose-hunting to stock up on jerky and pemmican for the winter: "It costs me about fifty dollars a month for food up here." He mentioned that he had no water, no power, no cable, but he did have a radio that worked on batteries, "unpolluted water, lots of game, wild chickens [probably spruce grouse], rabbits, all the fish I want any time . . . and NO TAXES. . . . I am really getting out of this city life and will reside here at Birch Portage."

Around this time, Augie phoned me to announce that he was coming to Saskatoon to stay with some friends. At last we would meet face to face and shake hands. He would phone me when he got settled, and we could go out for a bite to eat. A lot had happened to him during the spring and summer. There had been some break-ins at his cabin, and one of the culprits was a bear that laid waste to the cabin's interior, ate his food and part of his manuscript.

"A bear ate your manuscript?"

"Oh, yeah, Davey. A big black bear."

About to leave for Prince Albert for yet another funeral and wake, Augie had not been able to lock his cabin. Instead, he hammered an 8 × 4.5–inch strip of plywood across his door. The bear had smelled food inside and ripped the plywood off the door.

"Yeah, he really went to work. He tore up the inside of the cabin, ate up the food. Hey, that bear, he even ate up the canned food. Scattered the flour and the sugar all over the floor and scattered all my clothes and blankets on the floor, like with all that flour. And the roof wasn't finished, eh, so the rain fell over everything for the six weeks I was gone, and the bear and the rain, they destroyed about one hundred pages of my story. One whole month's work, eh. Then some guys come in and stole my stuff."

"The roof wasn't finished? I thought your cabin was nearly done."

"Oh, well, I had a bit of work to do, ah? But there was this funeral."

But there was this funeral.

I began to fill in the blanks. A six-week funeral meant a lot of drinking. In this case, it also meant two weeks in hospital (I didn't ask). And after our phone call, I began to wonder who would show up in Saskatoon, the reformed drinker bursting with new resolve to finish his story, or the despairing man who had fallen once again into a bottle.

Augie phoned me in Saskatoon, the following spring.

"I thought we were going to meet last fall."

"Oh, Davey, I guess I couldn't make it. But here I am."

It was a warm spring day in 2004, and I had heard about some of his medical problems, including type two diabetes.

"How are you feeling, Augie?"

"Oh, Davey, I'm ridin' high today. Just won a fortune at the casino."

Oh, Jesus, Augie was drunk again.

"You gotta come down here, Davey. Have a drink with me."

With great reluctance, I agreed. I simply had to meet this guy in the flesh. I drove to a sports bar south of town on Lorne Avenue, where people could eat, drink, gamble, and watch boxing and hockey on the big screens. I found Augie sitting at a table with several other guys. He rose, we shook hands, and he embraced me like a brother.

"Oh, Davey, you're such a good guy," he said.

We found a table on our own so that I could throw some questions his way.

"Augie, could we talk about Brer Lepeigne? Are you okay with that?"

"Ahhh, that guy was a sonofabitch."

"Remember when you and your friend caught sight of him in The Pas?"

"Davey, that guy was a real sonofabitch, eh?"

"But what did you do when—"

"Ohhhh, Davey, you're such a great writer. I'm lucky to have you as a friend. You're such a great guy."

"But Augie, what about my question?"

"Davey, you ask me any question you want. Lemme buy you a drink."

It was a short night. We didn't talk again until the fall of 2004, and this time it was by phone. He was in Prince Albert, and he sounded subdued.

"I think maybe I got to quit drinkin', Davey. Can't go on this way."

"I think you're right, Augie."

He paused for a few seconds. "You think so?"

"Yes," I said, "because when you're drinking you don't seem to hear my questions. You don't seem to listen to me, Augie."

This time there was a longer pause, a grave moment drifting between us, because I think Augie was hoping for another answer from me. I'll never forget that phone silence, and I can't help wondering if this moment gave

Augie, for the first time, an inkling that I might be judging him.

His letters that followed, however, betrayed none of that gravity or uncertainty about the status of our friendship. He wanted me to think of him as a "best friend." His first letter in 2004 contained copies of some forms he had to fill out for his lawyers. One line reads, "I AM NINETEEN YEARS OR OLDER." Augie complained about this line to me. "I see that they got my birth date wrong." He has crossed out the word "nineteen" and printed in "74 SEVENTY FOUR." One of the forms asks Augie about his work experience. It began officially in June of 1947 when he started working for the Churchill River Power Company at age seventeen. "It's a long story, Davey . . . [but] I was still driving taxi when I retired at age sixty-seven."

Joseph Auguste Merasty, power company employee, taxi driver, fisherman, hunter, trapper, labourer, visual artist, memoirist. Like many a memoirist before him, Augie seemed eager to rescue some of his key experiences from the ravages of time. By the late summer of 2005, when Augie had finished building his cabin and was about to resume work on his memoir, he wrote, "I feel like a man on death row. I'll be seventy-six in January but I still work hard and walk a lot, and I don't drive and I eat right. I'm on special diets, hoping to add a few more years to my stay here on this planet. . . . Someone once stated that the only way to achieve some semblance of . . . immortality [is to] do some painting or write a book and you will be remembered for all time after you kick the bucket. Well, in a way that is one way of looking at . . . the afterlife, EH WHAT."

He told me that his spouse had recently passed away. He frequently referred to the dozens of funerals he'd had to attend between 2002 and 2005, but I was not aware that he had found someone since his romantic disaster of 2002, let alone lost his partner. These insistent whispers of mortality must have infused him with a greater resolve to get healthy, do his art work, and write his book.

I suspect that much of what he wrote reached his lawyers, but not very much found its way to my mailbox. The exception to this lengthy lapse, of course, was his letters to me, which had taken on an urgency and a hint of hope for his final years. He had almost quit the boozing entirely (but not quite), he had become an outspoken critic of cigarette smoking, he was still hunting moose and making pemmican, still fishing through the ice, and, as I reported above, he had at last finished his cabin.

In the late summer of 2005, he began his letter to me in high spirits: "Well! Hello David O'boy, I suppose you may have thought I must have passed on . . . well, I haven't been all that healthy . . . in the past year and maybe [I've been] a little overworked at times. I have been building on my property at Birch Portage for the last six summers, and I did it all alone. I wanted to do it that way." In previous letters, Augie had lamented the many times people had broken into his cabin and stolen his tools and other personal possessions. But when he had returned to the cabin in that spring of 2005, "lo and behold, I only lost a rod and reel and one hammer this time."

Augie was feeling the weight of his years, but his fatigue was now that of the hardworking man looking back on his life from his childhood in Pelican Narrows to his adult life as a paid-in-full member of the working poor. By this time, Augie had conditioned himself "to accept the inevitability of the end of [my] life here on this planet, that no one gets out of this world alive." And once again, when I read these words, I thought, *What resiliency!*

Late in the winter of 2006, Augie wrote me about the challenges of staying sober and healthy at age seventy-six. For some time he had been without a vehicle, so for several summers he hitchhiked from his cabin at Birch Portage to Prince Albert, a distance of 270 miles, "starting about two hours before sunrise, and I usually walk ten to fifteen miles before getting rides (ten to thirty miles per vehicle). I counted the mileage. Last summer I walked thirty-four miles [between rides] before getting to Prince Albert, a total of seventeen to eighteen hours, but I made it. Would a smoker do that?"

Augie wrote this with obvious pride, but his hard life had taken its toll. "I take pills daily and nightly for high blood pressure, diabetes, bladder and prostate gland, stomach and sleeping pills, even Tylenol #3 for two fractured ribs when I slipped on the ice two months ago." And on the possibility of publishing his memoir, he had become aware that he would be "despised by many" who would read what he had written, but he assured me, "I can live with whatever anyone thinks or does to me. It is as simple to die as it is to be born."

Things had come to a head for Augie. 2006 was the year that the first of his payments would come to him from the residential school claim. This was the year that Augie became vocal about all kinds of issues. This was the year that his written testimony would be read. As I mentioned earlier, Augie wrote this testimony on behalf of many others who had spoken at the commission hearings but who had written nothing down.

After that 2006 letter, it was a long time before I heard from Augie again. By this time, I had received only a part of the testimony that he had sent to the Merchant Group of lawyers who represented him, but by my reckoning, the stories he sent me had brought me to the very heart of his experience as a student at St. Therese Residential School, and his eight long letters to me went a good way toward telling his story of moving on into adulthood and old age. In other words, I had a record of his life in school and a record of the sometimes chaotic, sometimes heroic aftermath of his life. But I had hoped to receive more.

I wrote letters to Augie, but not one was answered. As the years passed, I wondered what I should do. Edit what I had with me and make it into a book, or wait for more material? I decided to wait. In the meantime, I finished a book of novellas entitled *Welcome to Canada*, and continued to work on my own memoir, *A Hunter's Confession*.

Finally, in March of 2009, after three years of unexplained silence, Augie wrote to me, his ninth letter, and, as it turned out, his last. He was seventy-nine now, and had been using the money from his Truth and Reconciliation Commission payments to help some of his family along. Augie sounded once again as though he were full of good things.

> I will be very busy until about October, moose hunting in September to get ready for winter (dried meat, pemmican, etc.), and I have decided to remain dry until Christmas at least and will probably stay at the cabin most of the

time, writing, painting, and living and eating off the fat of the land, as they say. I know that being sober is the only way I can go back to my original way of life. I feel I have wasted at least twenty-five years or more of my life, and God-given talents, and I don't really have that much time left unless I smarten up.

In this letter, Augie enclosed a few pages of material from his residential school stories, some of it rewritten from earlier times. The writing was as succinct and lucid as it had ever been in the eight years he had been corresponding with me. He promised me about sixty-five more pages. So, once again, I waited. Life took over. I began a new novel. My wife and I did some camping, my son and I did some hiking in the mountains, my buddies and I went fishing. I resumed work on Augie's memoir. I finished a draft of my novel. Again, my letters to Augie went unanswered.

And then in November 2013, my wife and I went down to the Stegner House for retreating artists in Eastend, Saskatchewan, she to work on her paintings for a month, me to finish the job on Augie's work that he and I had agreed on more than a decade ago. Somehow I was sure that Augie was gone and that he would never see the work I had done on his memoir. But I hate to give up on anything, and I had promised him that I would finish this work, even if the remaining stories did not show up.

I tried once again to find out what had happened to Augie. I phoned numbers he had given me in the past, and I sent out some letters to addresses in my Augie File. A helpful woman at the Indian-Métis Friendship Centre in Prince Albert promised to ask around for me. Sometime approaching mid-November she phoned me back.

"You were looking for an old fellow named Augie Merasty?"

"Yes."

"He's alive," she said. "He comes here every so often and sits across the room from my desk."

"He's alive?"

"He says he's over eighty years old."

"Do you have an address for him?"

"No," she said. "No one knows where he lives."

HERE IS THE STORY IN AUGIE'S WORDS. I'VE TIGHTENED up his style from time to time. I have eliminated some excess verbiage: for example, the instances where he simply repeats himself. Some of these changes came about from phone calls between Augie and me over the years. If some passages confused me, I revisited them with Augie and reworded the confusing parts according to the context of his remarks and his explanations to me.

I corrected Augie's grammatical lapses if they created any confusion or if they called undue attention to themselves. I had no intention of highlighting these lapses. For example, his "interment" became "internment," "cumberland house" became "Cumberland House," "there" became "their" and vice versa, and many commas turned into periods. My occasional additions of information appear within square brackets in the text.

As I have suggested earlier, rather than giving me a finished manuscript, Augie mailed me many enclosures. Sometimes, therefore, the same incident would be recounted more than once with some variations. I had to work out with him, and sometimes without him, which details to retain and which to discard.

The result is a coherent manuscript but with some questions still unanswered. Why, for example, did Brother Lepeigne hang around The Pas when he turned his back on his vows and left the school? Why did he not flee to a French community that might have welcomed him? Did he not anticipate that his life might be in danger? What happened to Lepeigne after Augie and his friend ran into him in The Pas?

As Augie's memories start to fade, as time moves on for all of us and plays its little tricks on our memories, as the planet follows the pull of its galaxy and the constant drift of our universe, we might well ask, *Where are we, really?* Sometimes I ask this question. The answers fade and certainty becomes relativity's ping-pong ball. Trying to pin down Augie with my questions yields intimations of this same cosmic uncertainty.

One of the things I keep noticing in Augie's written accounts is his fascination with the people who were his keepers. His curiosity about people took him well beyond simply praising or indicting them. Augie could have given me a point-by-point account of the atrocities at St. Therese Residential School and organized everything around the sordid facts of the case. But at times he moves beyond the bounds of accusation and judgement into the region of a true memoir. Sister St. Felicity's passion for young boys is mingled with affection. Brother Verwelkend's perversions can be seen in the larger context of his politics. Brothers Languir and Cameron's yearnings for teenage girls seem to be driven, in part, by loneliness and social isolation. Like Augie, I almost feel sorry for them.

These familiars of Augie are often presented to us in and for themselves—as though Augie is interested in his torturers and kindly keepers alike, beyond their assigned roles. He seems curious about the reality of their lives. This richness of detail that moves beyond the mechanics of mere condemnation is the most engaging part of Augie's work. He gives ample space to the nuns, priests, and brothers who were kind and considerate or just plain fun to be around. He has not only acquired a strong sense of moral outrage, but through his many ordeals he has also preserved a sense of fairness and demonstrated a perceptive intelligence. His memoir manages, from time to time, to rise above the sordid details and resentments of his incarceration to document the chaotic life around him.

I have read enough accounts of the atrocities of the Holocaust by such writers as Elie Wiesel or Primo Levi to realize the futility of comparing Hitler's atrocities to those of other violent and oppressive regimes. Augie might differ with me on this, but I won't fall into the trap of calling the moral travesties at St. Therese and the tragic consequences of Canada's experiment in residential schools for Aboriginal children our national Holocaust.

But sometimes, when I think about the complicity and the silence that came from respected clerics and churchmen in Hitler's Germany and Mussolini's Italy, that same silence and that same complicity resonate with Augie's long ordeal during virtually the same years in a church-run residential school. I am referring to the callous regime—the corporate structure, if you will—that hired and protected people like Sister St. Mercy at St. Therese School in Sturgeon Landing, the lessons she learned from Brother Lepeigne, the lessons she apparently taught to Sister Joy. And still in this disheartening vein, I am thinking of one of St. Therese's school principals, Father Lazzardo. In his livelier moments, he was an equal-opportunity thug, spreading his chaotic violence among boys and girls alike. And I think of jolly old Brother Johannes Verwelkend, selling swag for Hitler's war effort and spreading the gospel of *pohtitiyihiki* among the little boys who gathered around his sewing machine and his dangling testicles. Like Augie, then, I have been pondering the institutionalized strategies of silence that protected these ghouls and allowed them to pursue their violent recreations for so many years, swinging their corrugated hoses and their straps, rattling their clappers, and flourishing their candles to teach the children about the fires of Hell.

I'm not much interested in writing a tirade against the Roman Catholic Church in Canada. If you detect evidence of a tirade (and I hope you do), it is focussed on the predators and sadists who worked at St. Therese, their superiors who allowed them to carry on unchecked, their conspiracy of silence, and on a government that shares complicity with that system of residential schools in our country. As far as I have been able to discover, similar patterns of abuse have been uncovered relative to Canadian residential schools run by other churches.

Every winter I attend a writers' colony to work on my manuscripts. This colony gathers at St. Peter's Abbey in Muenster, Saskatchewan. I've come to know the priests and the monks who live and worship there, and I think of some of them as my friends. One of the abbey's monks was recently discovered to have been a child predator at a residential school some decades ago. He was expelled from the abbey, charged, sentenced, and imprisoned for these crimes.

Clearly something has changed for the good. And that change came about in part because people like Augie Merasty spoke out against their oppressors, and because various people started to listen. I cannot escape the conviction, therefore, that I am writing about a hero.

Recently, in our writing community, I have noticed a healthy increase in First Nations writers, and I am beginning to see a trickle of these writers come to our colonies at St. Peter's Abbey. Perhaps a day will come when these residencies at the abbey will have the same appeal for our Aboriginal writers as they do for non-Aboriginal writers. At the moment, most of the First Nations writers I know tend to feel more comfortable retreating in non-religious venues, like the Saville retreat centre in the Cypress Hills near Ravenscrag, Saskatchewan.

I hope that someday more of these First Nations and Métis writers will also feel inclined to retreat with writers of all stripes at St. Peter's Abbey, that they will no longer find any targets for their anger and nothing to fear, that the echoes of past oppression will grow fainter. If, as I suspect, the church pendulums have begun to swing in a salutary, inclusive, and compassionate direction, this progressive thinking may have come at the cost of Augie's innocence, not to mention that of thousands of boys and girls in this country. And perhaps this sacrifice has not been entirely in vain.

Well done, I say to Augie. *Good work.*

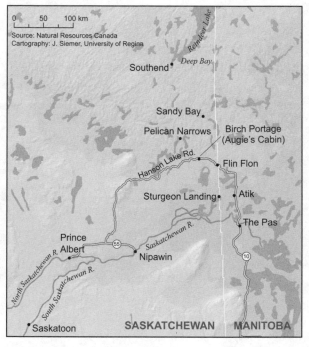

Sturgeon Landing and other places discussed in this book.

ONE

School Days,
School Days

AROUND THE 26TH OF AUGUST, 1935, MY FATHER
decided it was time for us kids to be taken to Sturgeon
Landing by canoe, which was propelled by a four horse-
power motor. It took several days to get there on the
river. We had to reckon with a dozen rough rapids and
eight portages. Two or three of those were about three
quarters of a mile long, with thousands of black flies and
mosquitoes to fight all the way.

In those days, the whole country was teeming with
northern wildlife, including fish of many kinds, which
my dad scooped out of the waterfalls with a scoop net
made especially for that purpose. We lost about twenty-
four hours of travelling time in all. My dad shot and
killed a bull moose, and we had to stay in one spot on the

South Sturgeon weir to smoke the fish and cut and dry the moose meat. Yet we got to our destination a whole day ahead of schedule.

I was born in 1930 at Sturgeon Landing and baptized there by Father Aquinas Merton, OMI, who was also the head administrator and principal at St. Therese Residential School from 1927, when the school was opened. Two of my sisters and my brother Peter were the first three to walk inside the school. Annie and Jeanette were the names of my two sisters. There were also six uncles and the same number of aunts who attended the school in its first year.

All those sisters and cousins, uncles, and many other unrelated people from other villages told me what had happened. Good and bad, positive or negative, were told to me and others when we got to school eight years later, and they all told basically the same stories. So one has to assume they were speaking the truth and nothing but.

A lot of their stories I already wrote and submitted to our lawyers, who number about thirty-six across Canada, representing the survivors of residential schools. The six that are working with me and others here in Saskatchewan have offices downtown in Saskatoon.

THE FORMER PRINCIPAL, Father Aquinas Merton, was the hardest working man that I have ever known. Well, he was not like the next one. It was just the opposite with this kind and friendly principal, Father Bernard Pommier. He never touched a plow or any farm implement, and I honestly could say I never even saw him enter the barn. He was always super clean and wouldn't go into a smelly barn, let alone drive a team of horses or milk a cow, or shovel and scrape dung. No, sir, he always had to be immaculately dressed and really preferred to have all the privacy he could get. All of the boys who knew him can say the same, that we never saw him lifting a block of wood or anything from the warehouses.

Sometimes Sister St. Mercy, whom I will write a lot about, would send some young student upstairs to the principal, assuming the Father would take care of him one way or another. But instead, Father Pommier would ask the boy why she sent him to see the principal.

"Oh, well, I was laughing a little too loud in the washroom during lineup time."

Then he would start laughing himself and say, "Is that all you came to tell me? Just a waste of my time and yours. Next time just laugh *kīmōc* [in English, "quietly"]. That is all I have to say. Now go back down to your classroom." More laughter from Father Pommier, "I'll talk to Sister Mercy later."

No one can ever say anything bad about this principal, Father Bernard Pommier. He was a far cry from the principal who took over two years after I left the school, Rev. Father L. Lazzardo. I will write about him later.

BUT BACK TO my story. Yes, in the fall of 1935, when I was only five years plus eight months, my father made arrangements with the principal, Father Aquinas Merton, to allow me to start schooling even though I was not of school age. I would be six in January 1936. Due to the distance from the residential school and the need to travel in winter by dog team in extremely cold weather, it would be very hard on a six-year-old child just to take him to St. Therese School. And that winter my father and family had decided to go way up north to trap. So they took me to school at the end of the summer when I was still five years old.

It was that fall that I first laid eyes on the one human I would dislike for the rest of my school term, if not for the rest of my life: Brer Lepeigne (pronounced "Le Pain"), who was there from before I arrived and stayed at St. Therese until 1939 or 1940. But I will not talk about him now. I want to keep talking about the nice ones.

I want to talk about my first class teacher for grade one. Her name was Sister St. Alphonse. Well, she was one of the kindest and most loving persons in that institution. She was also our boys' keeper in our playroom and joined us in playing Hide and Seek the Marble and other games we enjoyed. Once in a while, when some boy was extremely disobedient and wouldn't do what he was told to do, she would use the small ruler we kept at our desks and tap him on the palm of his hand very lightly, and we could see that both of her eyes were shedding tears, which she wiped with her white kerchief. It didn't happen too often. Since she taught in grades one and two, I was in her classroom for two school years. She never changed in her loving and kindly ways, and I'm sure she still is that way. I met her ten years ago in Nipawin, Saskatchewan, and she kissed me hard, bless her.

Well, I'll continue with this memory of all the sisters who showed kindness and genuine care for us kids, good or bad, and as I said aforehand, you did not have to do anything gross to be punished for bad behaviour at St. Therese Residential School.

Sister St. Famille was our baker at the school and also one very kind and loving individual, and every day or every other day, three or four boys were taken from the classrooms and told to help Sister St. Famille, who required a lot of manual labour when baking for about 120 people. She knew only a few words of the English language, so we had some difficulty communicating with her. Some words she always used when some kid got smart or noisy. With a half-smile she would raise her arm and wave her forefinger to and fro, and say, "Look boys no smarrrt, no bread."

The boy would not get her specialty that she called "La Galette," small round bannocks, which were really special to us, as we never were served bannock in our meals. It was always the same, bone-dry bread that raised heck with our gums and teeth. The Fathers, Sisters, and Brothers enjoyed beautiful white bread served by Sister St. Virginia Rose, who was their special cook. I swear, those people of this school administration would not even look at our bread or our food. To them it was puke.

Now, Sister St. Bonhomme ran the sewing room with help from six or seven girls. They did all the mending and made slippers and linings for our shoes in winter, and for our mitts, which, by the way, were made from old canvas and old, grey, horse blankets. Sister St. Bonhomme was also our keeper in the playrooms and the refectory (dining room). She was not too mean, except when we got too noisy and didn't heed her clapping. Whenever our keepers wanted to get our attention, they had what we called a clapper, a wooden two-piece item joined by hinges on one end and banged together with both hands, making a noise like a large woodpecker. Once in a while, though, Sister St. Bonhomme used a strap when she deemed it necessary. I still say she was one of the kinder nuns.

Then I'll talk about Sister St. Ange de Cachot, who was our nurse. There were two Sisters St. Ange de

Cachot, but this first one looked after the sick children and whoever got hurt at school. I can only say she was exceptionally kind and sympathetic. She really wanted to do whatever she could to ease the pain of whatever the problem laid. She once looked after us when the regular keepers were away.

There was Sister St. d'Amitié, who was mostly the girls' keeper but many times our keeper. She played with us and really enjoyed her time at our playroom. She loved doing us favours, like carrying love letters back and forth from our playroom to the girls' playroom. She knew full well she would get some kind of a reprimand if she ever got caught with what she was doing, but she never got caught. (Only one other nun did those letter deliveries, and that was Sister St. Doucette, my junior high school teacher, originally from the United States.) Sister St. d'Amitié was a cook's helper and girls' keeper, and was never known to strike anyone in the school. The girls really enjoyed having her as keeper, especially when they got her to carry their love notes back to us guys.

I cannot remember the name of one of my second-grade teachers, who also taught the grade-four kids. I can only remember that we called her Old Bodo, because she looked so much like a guy who lived across the river here in Sturgeon Landing. She looked mean enough and she was very tall, and we had little chance of doing anything wrong, as she used the strap occasionally. It really made a kid cry, because she had a strong arm. But it did not happen very often once we got the story and saw what she could do with a strap. Otherwise, most of the time I can recall, she was a nice and kind old soul. Most of the time she was our refectory-room keeper. One can imagine the sound of 110 children all talking and laughing together. She didn't like to be called Old Bodo, but she was okay.

Sister St. de Mer was our Sister Superior from the time I entered St. Therese, and was there before I even arrived, until she was replaced by the other Sister St. Ange de Cachot. All I can say about both of those Sisters is that they were kind and loving in every way, and they never did anything to hurt anyone, never used the strap. That's all I can remember about these two Sisters. When they left sometime in the summer of 1942, and when we came back from the holidays, we sure missed them.

Here are some of the brothers who were good to us. Big Brother Beauville (we called him Big Beauville) is one of them. Brother Beauville was a good and jolly person. His work was mostly driving a team of horses and working inside the barn, which housed cattle and horses. He always smelled like cow and horse manure. He was a big overweight man, a kindly person who never said a mean word to any of the boys. He was always in a playful mood, but he never stopped working at a job he was ordered to do until it was done. On or about the winter of 1942, he was kicked in the face by one of the big horses that wore metal shoes on all four hooves, and one can only imagine what that could do to anyone. But Big Beauville was a big and tough individual. The blow could have killed a small person or crippled one for life. Brother Beauville, however, went to St. Anthony's Hospital in The Pas to have his battered face fixed and had to go back later to have it redone. He was absent for a total of two months. We missed him a lot, and we all prayed for him.

Now, there was also Brother Leopold, a tall, lanky, middle-aged, and very friendly man. He always carried a pouch of chewing tobacco. He drove a team of horses and, most of the time, a load of kids. He only stayed at the school for two school years, so I don't have much to say about him, except that he was a really kind person.

Then there was Brother Henri Jean, the engineer, who looked after the boiler room, making sure all the machines and the heating systems were in working order. He was one of the hardest working men at the school and a good engineer. About twenty of us boys worked with him every morning, filling the wood bins for the boilers. We also worked at taking the wood in for the kitchen and for the baking. Brother Henri Jean was at most times a kind and jolly old fellow. But occasionally, whenever us boys got disobedient or disrespectful, he would blow his baldheaded top and roar like a lion, throwing blocks of wood against the walls to make a lot of noise.

Brother Henri Jean was a stammerer. When he couldn't stand the horsing around, he would roar, "All right, you bastards. G-g-g-g-g-get out, all of you!" Otherwise, he was a very loving and kindly old soul when nothing bothered him. In all those years from 1927 to the time I got out in 1944, I have never heard of him breaking any rules or having a serious problem with the machinery he was supposed to maintain. I can only end up by saying, he was a great guy.

TWO

Hard Times

WE USED TO ENJOY GOING OUT MILES AWAY FROM the school, going on picnics, either to the beach or going fishing at the rapids north of the school. It felt so nice to get out of the enclosed playground. Most of the time, we were forced to stay within the yard, which was surrounded by a high barbed-wire fence. It felt like getting out of prison. But I recall many times I was detained and was not able to join the crowd going to these good times if I was penalized for whispering during silence, or poking someone in the ribs, or swearing in Cree, as I did several times. I once wrote down "I will not whisper during silence" five hundred times while everyone was gone out of the school area.

I really can't recall just how many times I was made to pay for such minor offences. I was once made to walk about twenty miles in −40°F weather with a fellow student, Abner Joseph, back to where we walked the day before, across the big lake with a strong wind blowing. I imagine the wind chill factor was about −60°F. Just because we lost one mitten each. We were very nervous and scared all the way, as we were only about eleven or twelve years old at the time. And we saw some fresh wolf tracks about six miles out on the lake and kept our eyes busy looking every which way, expecting to see some wolves following us. And we were only carrying sticks three feet long and two inches around. Not much defence against an animal like a wolf. We came back without the lost mittens as the wind and snow had covered everything that could be lost. That was January 1941, and it was that meanest of all nuns, Sister St. Mercy, who had forced us to walk in that godawful weather, only to come back empty-handed. We, of course, got the strap, twenty strokes on both hands.

Also my left eye still waters and aches where I was hit a number of times by two Sisters who worked for four or five years as boys' keepers. Sister St. Mercy again and Sister St. Joy, who was Sister Mercy's disciple. Sister St. Mercy trained her well, at different times. They really enjoyed causing pain and other kinds of suffering as punishment for the smallest infractions. I think they were paranoid in the position they had, being masters of a lower race of creatures, Indians, as we were called.

"Indians from the bush, what can you expect?" was Sister Mercy's favourite phrase.

They wanted to show who was superior, and no rule or order was to be broken or spoken against. They wanted to impress upon us that all this was for our own good and the will of God, and that the order of nuns, brothers, and fathers of the Oblates of Mary Immaculate (OMI) were to some degree servants of God on Earth, and we must take any punishment without complaints. To be disobedient was a sin in the eyes of God.

In the springtime when the cattle were mating, and all the animals were in the open yards, if we laughed too much or too loud while the bulls were doing their thing, we used to get whipped on the butts with a hose three feet long. We were chased away to another part of the schoolyard so we could not watch what was going on with the mating bulls and cows.

We also spent much time watching chickens and roosters doing what they did best. We were allowed to watch the chickens all we wanted without interference, and we used to make bets with whatever we had in hand—nickels, candy, or glass marbles, which the principal Father Aquinas Merton gave us occasionally. We used to make bets on how many times the rooster could mount the hens in thirty minutes. We all kept tabs. One white rooster did it nine times within thirty minutes. It was one of the lighter entertainments we enjoyed many times without interference or punishment.

During the nine years I was at school at St. Therese, even though all those chickens laid eggs, not one student ever once tasted one egg at mealtime. I was once caught with three eggs I picked up outside the chicken yard where some wandering hens laid, and was made to eat them raw, right in front of my fellow watchers. Brer Lepeigne must have thought we had gone right into the chicken coop to steal from the hens.

Every morning at breakfast, we ate rotten porridge and dry bread that was hard as cardboard. We always watched an impeccably white-clothed cart eight feet long being wheeled to the Fathers' and Brothers' dining room. Right through the centre of the refectory for all us boys and girls to turn and watch, licking our chops, all the beautiful food going past us ten feet away. It happened almost on a daily basis. Our keepers, one on the girls' side and one on the boys' side, banged on their clappers, and we were told to get back to our porridge and don't turn our heads again or it would be detention or another kind of penance.

Sometimes on feast days like Christmas, Easter, New Years, and other Saints' feast days, we saw even nicer food being wheeled by. It was absolutely gorgeous, especially when we were eating rotten fish or other distasteful crap. Especially during the Bishop's visit (Rev. Martin

Lajeunesse). On these days we all saw roast turkey, or steaks, roast chicken, doughnuts, and cake. Fresh cake. We used to drool and sigh, and of course we were ordered to get back to our rotten food. "Eat or I'll make you eat it, one way or another."

I always wondered why our keepers and teachers talked about Jesus, Mary, and Joseph and all the love they had for mankind, and Jesus being born in poverty, extreme poverty, and we should try to emulate him and learn to take punishment for our wrongs to pay here on Earth and not later in Hell or Purgatory. Apparently they didn't know it was suffering enough to see all that beautiful food being wheeled by and only getting a smell of it. I know they never practised what they preached, not one iota. Do to others what you want them to do unto you. Be kind to others. Jesus will love you for it, and so on, and on and on and on, all the talking and preaching in church and classrooms. And what they did to us and how they administered their little regime did not mean a thing to them. They never really practised what they preached, period.

Whenever there were visits of Bishop M. Lajeunesse or visits from chiefs or members of council from any Indian reserve, they used to make us dress in our best clothing, provide concerts, and they even served us some edible food, beef stew or something. And they treated those northern visitors with good food and everything nice, and of course that chief or counsellor would get up at the end of the concert and speak from the stage facing all 110 children, telling us how lucky we were to be looked after in such a school as St. Therese Residential, and we should be thankful to God and to the administration for such blessings.

Oh, God, I used to think, *what hypocrisy*. Somebody sure pulled the wool over their eyes, because that is how it was meant to look, and it happened time after time.

Sometimes for punishment we were made to kneel on the cold cement floor from 8:30 p.m. until almost midnight, after everyone had gone to bed upstairs. We would fall asleep on the cold cement floor before Sister Mercy came or sent for her co-worker Sister Joy to tell us to go to bed upstairs. Then we were woken up early in the morning to go to church. We were usually awakened at 7:30 a.m., like it or not. All we used for toothpaste was salt, which the sister carried in a saucer. Salt, something we didn't even get to use at mealtime. Yet the cows and horses were getting all they wanted in blocks in the fields.

These incidents I have written about happened many times, and I have long lost count of the number of times they happened, but it was the same thing, punishment and abuse over and over again, even before these two nuns and others abused me.

THREE

The Passion
of Sister Felicity

WHENEVER THE NUNS WENT ANYWHERE OUT OF the school, whether to go to the graveyard half a mile away or across the river, they always travelled in groups to protect themselves from harm. Our complex was a very large building, five floors in all, one side for males and one for girls and nuns. Inside the school with all of us in our classes, when a nun decided to fetch something or work on the boys' side, she was always accompanied by one or two older girls, presumably to avoid molestation or worse. That was the Sister Superior's rule. No Sister should walk alone around any part of the men's section at any time.

Now I know the reason why. No hanky-panky. They were all human beings, and they all had human feelings and weaknesses. Once I spent the whole afternoon with

Sister St. Felicity, who, by the way, was part Indian. She was at my school when it opened in 1927. Later, she went to the Medicine Hat Nuns' Academy and came back around 1942 to join the other nuns at St. Therese. By this point there were fourteen nuns.

I was a fairly good artist at age fourteen and did some fancy work on the principal's canoes, which he used when he travelled over the open lake all the way to Cumberland House, approximately forty miles away. Once Sister Felicity and me spent all afternoon in a private room while the others were miles away on a picnic. We were alone in that room, doing some art work.

After about an hour, she started scratching her leg, and now and then touching my right hand with her knuckles, and talking to me. She seemed to be in a nervous state, and when she asked me if I had ever felt some temptation when I looked at the girls, her face turned red. I told her that when we looked at the girls, we didn't have much chance for that.

About ten years later, well after I had come out of school, I heard from an uncle that, way back around 1929–30, in the same school, Sister Felicity had been his girlfriend. Once it happened that they made a date, by letter of course, to meet in a darkened place between the laundry room and the boiler room in the basement of the school. This old man is still alive at ninety-three years of age, so out of respect, I decline to mention his name. And I decline to write down what he told me as to what transpired between them in that darkened cubby hole between the boiler room and the laundry room. But he always told us with sincerity that Sister Felicity was no virgin, even all the time she was at the nunnery in southern Alberta.

So, getting back to my story with Sister Felicity and me that afternoon in the locked private room, she started raising her long black Sister's dress to expose her big white knee cap.

She took my right hand and said, "Augie, please scratch my knee. I'm going to be busy with both hands."

She was folding some art work or something. I started to flush myself as I never touched a grown lady's knee cap before.

I did it several times with the many girls my mother raised, orphans of uncles, aunts, and of army draftees who went to war, but that's another story. I really enjoyed all those shenanigans with all those girls and cousins at bedtime, way out in the wilderness where my parents lived in summer to fish commercially, but all that might get told at another time.

Back to Sister St. Felicity. I tried to retract my hand but she gripped it tighter and, holding my hand, lifted her dress way up to her thigh, exposing more white leg, and for every stroke of hers and my hand, I relaxed my tension and she really went at it, stroking harder and harder until I could actually feel her underpants. Then she let go of my hand, and with her left arm pulled me to her face. I quickly turned my face to the left and she smacked her wet face on my right cheek while pulling my right hand with her right hand. Her hand was large, heavy, and strong, so she had no trouble pressing my now very relaxed hand right into her crotch, though not inside her pants. She kept rubbing my hand against her vagina and I felt the wet of her underpants. "You're cute, Augie. Come on, let's see if you can come on." She made a grab for my penis, which didn't come erect because of shock and embarrassment.

Just like before, I still liked and respected her, but now in a different way. And she always favoured me for some reason, maybe thought I was an easy mark, and as before, she asked my teacher if she could work with me someplace.

When I think about that time, I wish it would happen again, right now. I guess I hesitated for too long.

Anyway, back to the story. I finally mustered enough courage to pull my hands back and stood up. I told her that I had to go to the washroom. She had a face as red as a beet, almost apologetic.

She said to me with tears in her eyes, "Be a good boy. You're the best. Please swear that none of this is told to anyone. I'll do you lots of favours. I'll get you candies, food, and I'll carry your letters, and your friends' love letters. But if you tell about this, no one will believe you. It will have drastic consequences and probably get a big rebuttal from the other nuns.

"I am sorry the Devil almost got the best of me," she added. "Thank God nothing more happened. And please keep your promise."

With that, she kissed me on the cheek and said, "Thank you, bye for now."

I did keep my promise for personal reasons, until years later when me and my uncle exchanged stories way after the war in the 1940s.

For Sister Felicity, I've always felt a close friendship because of the fact that she was a Cree and she spoke it fluently. When all this happened that afternoon, I was five months past my fourteenth birthday, and surely I could have produced more than what I did that day. She was someone I liked and respected, and it was more than easy to forgive. So I never brought it up until years later, after I heard about her passing. She was married at the time of her death.

By the way, she moved away from St. Therese one month after the incident with me. It was time for summer holidays, can't remember if she moved before or after them. I can't remember, but I never saw her again.

FOUR

The Loves of Languir and Cameron

THERE WAS ONE BROTHER LANGUIR WHO CAME TO St. Therese's from Montreal in about 1942. He had a prominent protruding chin, and all the older boys called him Long Chin or, in French, *Long Menton*. He scarcely spoke a word of English. To everyone he was the butt of laughter, a person victimized by all who associated with him at work or play. Apparently he had read some history of what Indians used to do in the past to whites, and he thought northern Indians, which we were, would act toward him like brutal savages. And some of the brothers warned him never to trust any of us. So we played many a joke on him. It took him a long time to get over his nervousness when he came down to the boys' room or joined us at play on the playground.

At first the bigger boys would surround him and poke him with their fingers, or start pushing him back and forth. His eyes would start to bulge and roll. He would say, "Excuse me for a minute," in French, of course, and he would start running like the devil was after him, turning his head back before entering the door of the school and into the office of Principal Father Merton, and telling him with tears in his eyes that those savage Indian kids were trying to hurt him. The priest laughed, of course, at his fears, and told him he had to get used to the boys' antics and playful ways. It took him the next two years before he became less timid, but it seemed he never trusted any one of us, especially when we were crowding too close to him.

He was always waving at girls on the playground, jumping up and down, howling, and calling the name of Jitty Dorian, who was always his favourite girl in his wishful mind. And he really loved and favoured her only brother, Cyril Dorian. Cyril and his pretty sister Jitty were Métis people from The Pas, Manitoba. We all knew that Brother Languir was madly in love with Cyril's sister. No matter what Cyril did to him, Languir never reported on him. Once Cyril grabbed Brother Languir between his legs and squeezed his testicles and made him howl so loud that this Brother broke loose and ran screaming into the school. Cyril disliked him very much, especially when Languir called him *nīstāw* ("brother-in-law" in Cree), which was the only word he knew in the Cree language. And he only knew "yes" and "no" in the English language. Languir was totally French. He never learned not to ogle and point toward the girls' yard, with his eyes rolling. He never stopped mumbling Jitty Dorian's name, at which Cyril Dorian would punch him in the face.

There was the time when Cyril was working with him in the barn when he jabbed Languir on the back of the foot behind the heel with a pitchfork. I heard the yelping and screaming as he came limping out of the barn, crying.

"Cyril, Cyril, Cyril! No no no!"

Languir ran limping toward the school infirmary, with blood oozing out of his heel, still crying. Cyril stood at the open barn door, holding the pitchfork and laughing.

"That should keep his mouth shut about my sister," Cyril said. "I'll kill him one of these days."

It was a long time before Brere Languir asked to work with Cyril again. He had made Languir cry so many times, which I saw with my own eyes, and yet Languir never once reported Cyril to Father Lazzardo or any of his superiors.

Once I shot Brother Languir in the back with a slingshot using dry beans. It couldn't have hurt too much, but that time I was beaten by Father Lazzardo with the strap, beaten with fists to the face, and a foot to the ribs. I will never forget how it hurt. If it was Cyril who did that to Languir, he would have just laughed and patted Cyril on

the back, never mind reporting the action to Father Lazzardo. Nothing that Cyril did wrong mattered to Languir.
He loved Cyril and his sister Jitty. He had a desperate love
for her, and I am sure that they both hated him, partly
because he was ugly with his protruding chin. But so it
went on for the next few years until both Cyril and Jitty
stopped coming back to school and stayed home in The
Pas. Presumably they were both over the age of fourteen.
It wasn't long after, when summer holidays came around,
June 1942 or 1943, that Brere Languir quit St. Therese
Residential School, and according to the grapevine, he
hung around The Pas until Jitty got married to another
man, and then Languir went back to Quebec.

THERE WAS ALSO a Scottish fellow, a bachelor as we
always called him, and who preferred to be called as such.
His name was William "Scotty" Cameron, and he had
a crushing feeling of love for a distant cousin of mine,
Loreena Campbell. His feelings were just the same as
those of Languir for Jitty. Desperate loves they could
never hope to get, as both were much too old and ugly,
to say the least, and I swear, and many would agree, that
Loreena Campbell and Jitty Dorian were the prettiest
girls at that time, with fair skin and upturned noses and
light brown hair. Halfbreeds, we call them.

Mr. Cameron did the same thing as Brother Languir. In the morning, at the time of Communion, when we all got up to receive the holy bread at the front of the altar and returned to sit back down in the pews, there was no doubt in anyone's mind as to what these two were thinking. Forever praying for something to make their wishes come true, as we were often told by Scotty Cameron. Me and one of my brothers were very close to our distant cousin, the pretty Loreena, and very often we were asked to help Scotty Cameron with the wood or asked to haul the hay from miles away. His theme was often expressed like this. He would let out a loud *Whoopee!* and look up at the blue sky and cry out, "Oh! If I had a team of horses, two acres of land, and, God willing, Loreena Campbell, I'd be all set."

That is the way it was with those two wishful thinkers, Languir and Cameron. Loreena Campbell got married at Pelican Narrows before she was seventeen, about 1947, and I was out of school for about three years by then, and I can just imagine how Mr. Cameron felt when he heard about the marriage. I hope he was relieved that he had lost her forever, and accepted what was probably inevitable.

I met Mr. Cameron twenty-seven years later at the old folks' home in The Pas. We talked about old times at the school, and of course he asked me how my cousin Loreena was doing. I told him how many kids she had, and that she was at her husband's trapline about six to eight months of the year. Mr. Cameron wiped a tear in his eye and whispered, "I guess the good Lord meant it to be that way," and that was the last time I saw him. I couldn't help feeling sorry for him even then. No doubt he ended his days pondering what might have been.

So much for Languir and Cameron and their desperate longings for someone beyond their reach. They both endured four or five years of misery until the girls left school for their villages.

FIVE

Brotherly Love
and the Fatherland

THERE WAS AN OLD GERMAN BROTHER BY THE NAME of Johannes Verwelkend (pronounced Fair-Velkend). He was about sixty-five years old when I started school, and he had been there since 1927 as a shoemaker. He was given a shoe-repair shop directly above the blacksmith shop where he worked with a big machine on the heaviest of rubber and shoe leather. Some of the things my uncles told me about him before I arrived at the school were a little hard to believe. Then I met him.

He liked to be surrounded by a bunch of boys from the youngest to the oldest at his machine. My uncles had warned me not to get too close to Brother Verwelkend, as he was a bad example to all boys, and he always seemed

THE EDUCATION OF AUGIE MERASTY

to enjoy what the boys were doing to him. He took the blue ribbon for bad example for little boys. Here is a story about him.

My uncles and others had told me that Brother Johannes, as we called him, used to tell a group of boys that there was nothing wrong with a little *pohtitiyīhikī*, which is Cree for corn-holing or sodomy, and he was still saying those words when I got there. Sixty-five years or so later, I still have a lot to say about Johannes Verwelkend.

Apparently he never wore any underwear or shorts of any type, not when he went to work in his shop, which was only two hundred feet from the school. We all found this out and discovered as well that he would deliberately slit his black pants between his legs, about eight to ten inches, right at the crotch area, and let his testicles hang out to air, as he often told us boys. He could not stand to keep them in, they got too hot or something. Of course, we boys believed whatever he said.

A couple of boys used to love to squeeze his bag to the enjoyment of Brother Verwelkend, who was loving every squeeze. Every now and then the man would let out a low moan and then a great howl, and tell the boy squeezing his nuts to take it easy. "Not too hard, please, go ahead and touch me but don't do it too hard." Lots of other boys, even the bigger ones, also got a lot of kicks from squeezing his testicles. "Easy," he would urge his boys, laughingly, if not lovingly. "Not too hard, please, not too hard."

This happened almost on a daily basis, and yet he went to receive the sacrament of Holy Communion every morning with the rest of the sisters and brothers. In my book, he was an emeritus of immorality, and no doubt he had an everlasting impact on many young boys. There very well may have been others in the administration with the same habit, but things were kept under cover.

He used to hold at least one of the boys back to stay with him after we were gone to school. Like other brothers who worked there, he had the authority to keep a boy in his workshop to help him with his work. One can only imagine what went on after everyone had left the shoe-maker's to go to classes.

I know for a fact that two of those young boys, who were usually held back to help Brother Johannes, learned all about *pohtitiyihiki* in Brother Verwelkend's shop. He once asked me to come to his shop if I wanted some candy. But after seeing those boys pulling his testicles and penis, I suspected that he was up to something, and I was afraid to be alone with him.

I don't know why this man was not reported to the authorities. I don't know if these boys reported Verwelkend to the Truth and Reconciliation Commission. I hope so. I can only guess how harmful he was to a lot of us boys.

If any of our teachers ever claimed that there was no evidence of sodomy in the school, they were lying. There is no doubt that these things were forced upon many of us at St. Therese in those days. A lot of kids suffered everlasting effects, and no doubt some effects have been carried right to the grave.

Six weeks before World War II broke out in September of 1939, Brother Johannes Verwelkend took leave from the school. And where do you think he went? He went overseas to Berlin. I will tell you the things I heard about his trip.

When Brother Johannes came back about the third week of August, 1939, he told us that he had finally met and talked with Sister Therese Neuman, who was quite famous to us school kids. We were told in our classrooms that she had imposed a lot of suffering upon herself and was thin as a rail, because all she ate were the little round hosts at Communion every morning, and she drank only water every day. She fasted for days and weeks, which was hard to believe, but in those days we all believed in miracles.

Brother Verwelkend went on to talk about, presumably, something he could not get out of his chest. Whenever we asked him what transpired between him and Sister Neuman, he kept saying, "*Ach*, she's crazy." *Ach* is a German way of registering disgust or anger.

"She's crazy. You know what she told me? I was surprised when she called me by my name. That crazy woman told me, 'Johannes Verwelkend, you shall never see the kingdom of Heaven unless you give your life and soul to God, and repent for your sins and do penance, like I do. Not so much for your own redemption, but for people like you. For people like you.' That's what that crazy woman told me. *Ach.*"

When Brother Johannes came back from Germany, he brought back three suitcases full of German-made mouth organs, mouth harps, and all kinds of trinkets to sell to us and to the people in the community. He told us little boys that the money he made would all go back to Germany. In the school there were two grandfather clocks with swinging pendulums you could hear from the outside when they struck the hour. Brought back from Germany by Brother Johannes, those were no doubt paid for by the school board, and also several cuckoo clocks around school offices. But all the money he received from selling those instruments and clocks went for the German war effort. I believe that everything he did was unbelievably vile and evil, even more than I could have comprehended back then.

He had sworn to uphold and adhere to all Christian principles, for God and country. But instead, he decided to give a helping hand to his former nation, which was at the moment planning to take over the world. Brother Verwelkend used to get a German newspaper that no one else could read. Verwelkend was a Hitler worshipper, a complete fascist. He always told us kids that Hitler and the Germans were the smartest people in the world, supreme above any other race.

Whenever any of us said anything bad about the German race, or about Adolf Hitler and his troops during the war, he would really blow his top. His face took on the colour of red beets, and we feared that he would have a heart attack.

"*Ach, ach,*" he would cry. "You people should know."

And he would chase us away and scream, "Get the hell out of my shop and stay out!"

Being just kids, we believed most of what he told us. If Germany won the war, he claimed, there would be peace on Earth for the first time ever. There would never be another war. But that never stopped us from saying all kinds of rotten things about his race.

Finally, one of the brighter older boys went to Father Aquinas Merton, the principal of the school, and told him what the brother was doing, selling musical instruments and sending money home to support Hitler and the German nation.

I cannot understand to this day why the people who had left the school and had become grown adults did not report Johannes Verwelkend to the authorities. Or report this perverted man to our principal. Granted, we all know now that there were hardly any laws in those days to prevent men from torturing us and causing us the pain we kids had to endure, much less laws to prevent child molestation, or regulations to get rid of men who presented a bad example to small kids.

I remember reading something in the Good Book. Jesus told the multitudes that it is better to tie a brimstone around the neck of a person and throw him into the sea, anyone who has corrupted or threatened the innocence of little children. Mind you, I forget the actual words, and maybe it was Abraham or someone else who said those words, but they are in the Bible.

But if ever there was a man who fits that description of corrupter of little boys or polluter of young minds (my guess would be seven hundred to one thousand boys), it was Brother Johannes Verwelkend. But I suppose that as long as he provided free help in what he was an expert at—repairing shoes, moccasins, and skates—the administration could turn a blind eye and a deaf ear. I could say more about this perverted so and so, but I believe this will do for now.

SIX

Father Lazzardo
among the Children

EVERY MORNING WE WERE MADE TO HAUL WOOD,
large logs for the boilers and smaller stuff for the kitchen,
which was located about two hundred feet away. We did
this for Sister Virginia Rose, who was a nice person but
a terrible cook. One morning Father Lazzardo was either
in a hurry or in a very bad mood. I was at the top of the
long stairway, approximately thirty or thirty-five steps
to the boiler room, and there were three other boys with
armloads of kitchen wood, and I had the large blocks of
wood for the boiler. I heard the door open behind me
and I didn't quite hear what Father Lazzardo was mumbling about. Now I can't recall if he did this on purpose
or pushed me to get out of the way. He was bringing into
the place a small table or chair or something.

All I can remember was waking up in the school's infirmary, a medical room we called it, with two hospital beds. I had a big gash in the back of my head on the left side. Soon I was taken to bed back at our dormitory. I should have been taken to St. Anthony's Hospital in The Pas, Manitoba, but they kept me in the dormitory for a whole month. I ended up with a headful of lice because I couldn't comb my hair or even scratch near the wound.

Right after my tumble down the stairs, I used to wonder, how long before I succumb forever or get operated on? All because of that injury caused by Father Lazzardo. I know now why I was not taken to the hospital. They were afraid I might talk too much and maybe expose the person who harmed me. And all the time I was in that dormitory alone and very lonely. I had my head bandaged, I was not supposed to scratch my head, and the lice were getting worse, and I just wanted to scratch my head so badly.

Another thing I can't forget. I have another scar on the front part of my forehead from being kicked hard by Brother Friedrich Gruenwald for whispering during silence in lineup time on our way to classes. I hit the sharp part of the door latch with my forehead from that kick.

These wounds on my head are still visible, and I will gladly shave my hair from those areas to prove it. Also the back of my right wrist. For the last sixty years or so I have felt awful pain, throbbing pain and headaches day and night on the left side and the back of my head. Also dizzy spells all these years and especially the last twenty or so.

Now, back to Father Lazzardo. I first learned this story from a cousin, who attended St. Therese's after I had left in 1944. By this time, Father Lazzardo had become the principal of our school. Father Lazzardo had trouble holding down his sex drive, which surfaced when he became the school principal. He had replaced Father Bernard Pommier. Sometime around the early 1950s, he asked the girls' keeper for two girls to come and clean his bedroom. As it happened, two of the huskier, heavy-set girls were sent to help the priest with this job. Both girls were fifteen years old. These were Angelina Robertson and Louise Deschambault (now dead). Angelina was sent across the hallway to clean Mr. Cameron's room, and Louise was given the order to clean Lazzardo's room about ten minutes later.

As some of us were told a few times by Angelina, while cleaning Scotty Cameron's room, she heard the sound of screaming and pounding on the walls, like someone getting attacked viciously. She dropped her things and ran to the room, whence this screaming for help had come. She said she kicked open the door and was shaken to see Father Lazzardo, half on top of Louise with one hand inside her dress and panties, and the girl screaming like a banshee. Angelina herself started to scream, at which time Lazzardo jumped off the girl, with one hand lowered to his fly, which presumably was open and ready for action.

He told Angelina to go and finish her work and wait for Louise. He closed the door with Louise still crying, and Angelina heard the Father telling Louise he was only playing, and he wanted to see what her reaction would be if things like this ever happened. He said for Louise not to tell anyone about this incident. Louise cried all that time in his room without doing any more work. Shortly after, he gave her a bunch of candy and some chocolates.

A long time before that, this same priest beat me with his fists until I bled from my nose and mouth, and kicked me in the ribs. He left us all with memories that we won't forget.

SEVEN

Sisters
of the Night

THE NUMBER OF TIMES ME AND MY FELLOW REPROBATES were made to kneel on the cold cement floor of the playroom long after everyone else had gone to sleep is lost in the span of time, but I know it was many times. Is that why I have such large kneecaps? When I was at that school, it seemed always to be winter time. The days of that time always seem to have been colder. Maybe it seemed so cold because we were so scantily dressed for winter. One pair of socks, one pair of thin wool slippers, and moccasins and rubbers. Once outside, even in −40°F weather, you were not let into the playroom to warm yourself unless you were crying and dancing, banging your feet on the ground when your toes were starting to freeze.

It was like that in Brer Lepeigne's time, and it was like that after his replacement, Sister St. Mercy, took over in 1939. I will relate a story about that sadistic nun, Sister Mercy. She must have been a student of Brer Lepeigne. As I mentioned before, I still bear some scars all over my head. She had watchful eyes. When she had on her bifocal prescription glasses, they added a tinge of dark beige colour, and her eyes looked twice as mean and twice as big. I cannot say enough to vilify her name.

She came to the school with a young nun, Sister St. Joy, who must have just come out of the Medicine Hat nunnery, and who was her bosom buddy and helper. In September 1939, Sister Joy became assistant boys' keeper and guardian, and it didn't take long for her to practise what her bosom buddy Sister St. Mercy was doing.

One night I was sleeping soundly after midnight when I was woken up by a horrible sensation. I thought I had lost my left eye. There was blood streaming down my face. Sister Mercy was holding her strap. She dropped the strap and ran to get a basin with water. She left her kerchief to hold on my eye and told me not to cry so hard lest I wake everybody in the dorm. Never did I see her as nervous and scared as she was at that moment. She was grieving as she washed my left eye and she couldn't stop repeating, "I'm sorry, very sorry, don't cry please." And she gave me a chocolate bar.

It had been her turn as a night watchperson, and when she heard me laughing and talking in my sleep, she didn't bother to find out what was really happening. Hit first and talk later. I got the corner edge of the strap, which was two inches wide and a quarter inch thick. The sharp edge of the weapon caught the corner of my left eye.

Of course, she used the strap on us every day, each morning before breakfast and always in the bathroom, anywhere from ten to twenty strokes on the palms of the hands, and more if you uttered any word or refused to hold your hand out to get the strap. Then you got strapped on the head and shoulders until you fell on the floor pleading not to be struck any more. And you had to promise to be of good behaviour from then on.

As we well knew, Sister Joy was well trained by Sister St. Mercy. But I have already told you that. I have talked enough about those two mean Sisters, but I might return to Sister St. Mercy later. But enough here of Sister St. Joy and Sister St. Mercy, because I am leaving the best for last. Or rather, the worst for last.

EIGHT

Lepeigne

SOME TIME AGO I SUBMITTED SOME ACCOUNTS OF what Brother Lepeigne did to me and to some of my schoolmates. Most of these actions happened when we were about eight to twelve years old, so I have not been able to remember everything from that time. But I remember more than enough.

Shorty Joseph (now deceased) was one of Lepeigne's targets. He told me that Brer Lepeigne used to ask him to touch his privates whenever all the boys were out playing. I can remember a few times that, when Shorty joined us to play outdoors, we could tell he had been through some pain, some abuse, and in all probability he had been forced to do perverted acts with Lepeigne. But we never dared ask Shorty. I figure now, as then, that he really got strapped to keep quiet about what transpired between him and Lepeigne. I have a lot more rotten things to say about Brer Lepeigne.

I mentioned before that I went to school when only five years and eight months old, which my father arranged with the principal, Father Aquinas Merton, because of the difficulty of travelling from north to south in the winter time when I turned six years old. Brother Lepeigne had been at the school since it opened in 1927, eight years prior to my entrance at St. Therese. At first he wasn't that mean to me, because I was the smallest kid of the fifty-five boys who were under his eagle eyes. His eyes and his nose, they both reminded me of an eagle, and he was quite mean and abusive to the older boys whenever he felt the urge to punish them for any little offence. He derived much pleasure from the screaming when he laid the strap to the boys. Some of them were stronger and harder to break, but that didn't bother Brer Lepeigne. If a boy didn't cry out loud when Lepeigne applied the strap or the flat board, he would bring out the corrugated, three-foot, garden hose, and that was for sure a guarantee to make him scream.

After I turned six years of age in January of 1936, he began to show some of his real feelings toward me. He may have harboured them in the first four months after I entered St. Therese, but he didn't bother to punish me for any misdeed at that time. Presumably he was waiting for me to become of school age, and then he could, according to the strict rules of the Catholic hierarchy, do what he wanted 'legally.'

He found many ways to punish us. If we farted while we were sleeping, we could get strapped right across the face. If we made the "dirty noise," as he called it, during lineup time, which always made us laugh or smirk, our misdeed might get us thirty or forty lashes of the garden hose. This made the victim scream in pain. If one of us pulled our hand away after the first two or three blows of his strap, which he swung with all the muscle he could muster, he would strike us on the head, face, and arms, and no stopping.

If Brother Lepeigne caught anyone whispering to another person or even smiling during silence time, or lineup time for church, classrooms, or bedtime, it was too bad for him. Lepeigne would stay hidden in some corner where the procession would walk by, and him knowing exactly where every boy would be placed in the lineup. He would swing the meanest of backhanders I ever saw. I felt his clenched fist more than once, and it was always followed with the same words.

"What did I tell you last night, Soweese?"

He had nicknames for most of the boys, and this was what he called me.

IT WAS BROTHER Lepeigne, from 1935 to 1939 or 1940, as I have stated before in the first part of my story about St. Therese Sturgeon Landing Residential School. At that time, and even now as I remember him, he was and still is one of the worst human beings I have ever known about, except maybe Hitler.

More than once, I remember, he wanted me to touch his penis. One of the times, when I was about eight and a half, I was in the same washroom with Lepeigne when everyone was out playing. I had to stay in because of a bad cold. He had tried to get me to touch his penis before by luring me up to the fourth-floor bathroom, but this time I thought I was safe. He may have even felt sorry for having tried this on me. After I finished urinating, he called me over to his toilet stall and grabbed my arm and pulled me in, telling me not to scream. He told me he'd give me candies and chocolate if I held his hard penis. He took me by the right wrist and grabbed my other arm and wrapped my little fingers around his hard penis and rubbed back and forth, masturbating himself. I felt his semen on my hand, and he still didn't let go until he made me swear not to tell anyone.

I started screaming, as if someone was trying to kill me. He held his hand over my mouth and almost choked me with his other hand and told me he would give me a beating with the three-foot garden hose if I ever told anyone. Then Lepeigne dragged me across the bathroom and threatened to throw me out the window, and I really believed him 100 per cent. I bit his finger and broke loose and ran out to play with the other boys.

From that day on I was detained upstairs in the dormitory every morning with about six other boys. I was made to lie on my belly on the bed while he swung the corrugated hose as hard as he could with the sole idea of putting fear into me to keep my mouth shut. That went on until he left about two years later. I figure I got at least five to six hundred beatings with that hose. The others too. If one of us rolled on the floor, Lepeigne would keep on beating him until he got back on the bed.

These beatings would happen after church, when everyone had gone down for breakfast. I figure now the reason he did what he did to me, all those whippings, was to keep my mouth shut about that sexual abuse. He did a good job, because I have never told anyone about those assaults, until now. They were too painful and shameful to me, and I would have been the laughing stock for everyone, even to this day.

I knew three boys, one from The Pas and two of my own relatives, who seemed to be Lepeigne's favourite targets. He always preferred to work with them or walk into the bush with them. These boys have all grown up with these nightmares, but only one of them is still alive.

There were other boys, like me, who hated Lepeigne, who could never forget the many beatings and back-handers from him. He knew, of course, who we were. We couldn't show any love or respect for such a demonic personality. Even now I wonder, why wasn't the Bishop's house ever told about these things? But as things were at that time, priests, nuns, brothers belonging to the order of the Oblates of Mary Immaculate were considered by all Catholics to be infallible, and they were respected with unshakeable reverence, especially by my parents, who were in my view, then and now, religious fanatics. They naturally believed that whatever was done to us, if we were properly disciplined, was for our own spiritual good.

NINE

Revenge

I WAS ONCE DETAINED BY SISTER ST. MERCY INSIDE the playroom, while everyone else was outside playing. She came in from the playground and asked why I was so disobedient and not a good listener, and she asked me if I believed in Hell or Purgatory. I didn't answer for a few minutes. She picked up something from her drawer and came toward me.

She said, "Get up and I'll show you something. I asked you if you believed in Hell or Purgatory."

I still didn't answer.

She said, "Put out your hand." Then she lit a candle and said, "Do you want to burn in Hell or Purgatory?"

I said, "Of course not."

"Put out your hand."

I put out my hand and she brought the candle close to my hand, and I started feeling the heat of the flame and started pulling my hand back.

"Unh unh," she said with a fiendish grin. "You don't like fire or heat. Well, Hell is a lot hotter than this. Better smarten up."

I and my buddies, six of the older boys of my age, about twelve- or thirteen-year-olds, developed such a hate of these sisters—St. Joy and St. Mercy—that we used to do some secret planning as to how we could get back at them. A good idea came when we were doing some sledding down the riverbank. Our river had open water running very fast, and it never froze in winter.

As me and my buddy Jayjay Deschambault were ready on the sled to shoot down the steep hill, to go down about forty miles an hour while my other close pals looked on, who do you think decided to catch a ride with us? Every one of my pals had something to say. Some suggested, now is your chance to get back at her somehow. Of course, we all talked Cree so she wouldn't understand what we had in store for her.

Patrick Doré said, laughingly, "Try to drown her in that rapids."

Benjamin Doré and Abner Joseph suggested we dump her just before we hit the rapids. I was at the very back of the sled as steersman, and I know something about sledding, but I made a move a little too late, probably two seconds too late. Anyway, the dumping went almost as planned. Everyone got off fine except the overweight Sister Mercy, who kept on rolling right into the fast-moving water of the river, and no doubt she would have kept on going right under the ice and would have stayed there until spring, except that there was only about fourteen inches of space between the ice and the sandy bottom in the rapids.

She got stuck between the ice and the bottom of the rapids. It took all three of us to pull her to safety. Her feet were somehow stuck tight under the ice. We had to help her up the hill, and we walked her to the school. She no doubt knew our prank was a deliberate act. Because it was.

After the incident with the slide we were all targets for more abuse and punishment for the most minor of infractions, and we weren't allowed to talk Cree whenever we were around Sister Joy or Sister Mercy. Somehow, and not without good reason, they came to the conclusion that the sled accident had not been an accident, but they never mentioned it. And we knew that sledding was never going to happen again.

As usual, we were forever conjuring up something dangerous or harmful on the platform where she always sat on her chair with her ever-watchful eyes. That chair always had a cutout carpet for a cushion. One day Patrick Doré brought a bunch of one-inch shoe tacks to the chair.

This was some months after the sled accident. We stuck the tacks through her carpet cushion with the points up to make sure at least some would penetrate as she set her heavy butt on the chair. She always seemed to sit down heavy every time. We waited with smirks and wry smiles as she came out of the hallway toward her favourite perch. Some of my buddies could not contain themselves. And then it happened. She sat smack down onto the chair.

I will never forget the piercing scream she let out and how she jumped up about ten times faster than she sat down. She was shocked for a second at the laughter from all of us, but she did not wait to ask. Just about then, Sister Joy came in, and in tears and in French she asked her to go upstairs and get the principal, Father Pommier, to come down and witness what happened. When Father Pommier arrived in the playroom and asked her what had happened, in French, with tears in her eyes and face as red as a beet, she explained.

The Father, too, was red-faced, and with a smirk, he told her to send the jokers upstairs. But how was Sister Mercy to know which jokers? So the smiling priest explained to the demoralized Sister St. Mercy that there was not much he could do until the culprit or culprits responsible were found and made to confess. And with that he said good luck and told Sister Joy, "See that she gets some medication if necessary."

I have no doubt he went upstairs laughing all the way, later telling all the other Fathers and Brothers about the incident. A little later all the brothers, the ones who were mostly friendly, could not help asking who was the guy that did that ghastly thing to poor St. Mercy. After they promised not to tell the principal, I told them it was Patrick and Jayjay who did it. They all laughed about it even months after the incident, even right up to the time I left school. It was no wonder that we were the prime targets for abuse and ridicule from Sisters Mercy and Joy.

Sister Mercy's favourite saying when something bad happened was: "If it isn't Auguste Merasty, it's Jayjay Deschambault. If not, it's Abner Joseph and the rest of the company. It's the dirty ones, the rotten ones, dirty fools."

BACK TO BRER Lepeigne, who from childhood must have been dedicated to preserve the French culture and to be supreme over his underlings, the lower classes, people whom he treated as his possessions. He managed to hurt us boys as much as he wanted to, and he got away with hardly any retribution or any other kind of payback. Brother Lepeigne did things that in this age he would be jailed for, and for a long time.

I was probably too young to grasp the story and the reason for his departure from St. Therese, but I suspect there were too many complaints to the top brass, and he became an embarrassment for the whole system. He departed with such a low profile, but I'm sure no one missed him when he left. For me and my friends, it was a glorious occasion to have him disappear from St. Therese Residential School.

I have to tell the following little episode because somehow it brought some semblance of justice. When Brer Lepeigne took eight of us to Sandy Beach, one mile west of the school, it was a warm spring day in June, just before the holidays. Some of the parents were around to take us home. Brer Lepeigne told us to strip, since there were no swimsuits to be had in all of St. Therese, and so we went skinny-dipping. Lepeigne probably only wanted to see our naked bodies. We were all under eight years old. We waded out waist deep. None of us knew how to swim.

He said to us, "I want you guys to hold your noses, tighten your mouths, and dive toward the shore."

It was about fifteen feet away. None of us moved. So he grabbed me and Shorty Joseph by the scruff of the neck and put our heads under water for a full ten seconds. He pulled us up gulping for air, and we all ran crying onto the beach. My dad was there. He was six foot four inches tall, while Brer Lepeigne was only about five foot three. My dad waded into the water, grabbed Lepeigne by the scruff of the neck, and put his head under water for about fifteen seconds.

I cannot let the story end here. I met Brer Lepeigne in The Pas. I was seventeen or almost eighteen years of age, and I had worked very hard for three or four years since I got out of St. Therese. I had trained with one of the best athletes that ever lived north of the fifty-third parallel, Roger Carrier. We paddled the whole summer long and built a sort of boxing ring and spent the whole summer boxing, wrestling, paddling. By the time I met Brer Lepeigne in The Pas, I was in tiptop shape, and he was in his fifties. I was with Jason Deschambault, another long-suffering victim of Brer Lepeigne. When we met up with him, I was rather under the weather. So we decided to give him the scare of his life for a change.

He told us that he was not a Brother any more. That was all I needed. We were staying at the Harvey Rooms, and about fifty feet from the rooming house there was a large abandoned ice house. I took Lepeigne by the scruff of the neck and we headed for the abandoned building. Me and my friend Jason reminded him of all the times he beat us up for no reason, and of the times he tried to molest me, and I told him it was time to turn the tables. I shoved a mickey of whisky down his throat and let it pour until he was choking, and he was on his knees begging for mercy. I told Jason in Cree, "Let's pretend we are going to kill him." We talked mostly in Cree, but in English we kept saying aloud, "Well, it's time to get it over with.

We can cover him up with all this sawdust. We'll be up north by the time they find his carcass."

I suppose we were both good actors, because the man got on his knees and begged for mercy, saying repeatedly, "You boys are Roman Catholics, you know you should not kill. It's the Fifth Commandment of God!"

"Oh, yes," I said, "but you didn't remember any commandments of God when you tortured us for almost five years."

Conclusion

I MENTIONED HERE IN THIS ACCOUNT AND AT THE meetings of the Truth and Reconciliation Commission back in Prince Albert how we were forced to go to Confession, Communion. To go to church we were woken up at 7:30 every morning to wash up and brush our teeth with the saucer full of salt Sister St. Mercy was holding—we had to dip our wet toothbrushes into the salt. And, of course, every night we had another church service called Benediction. It lasted right until the time to go to the dormitory, and when we got to our dorms, it was time again to say our nightly prayers, which lasted another fifteen or twenty minutes. Before prayers were over and done with, many of the small kids had fallen asleep. Sister Joy, who became almost as heartless as Sister Mercy, used to walk around the circle of praying boys kneeling down beside their beds, and she would lightly smack someone on the back of the head if he dared to fall asleep.

All I have stated about incidents regarding our keepers at St. Therese are absolutely true, and I can write a lot more that transpired inside and outside of school. But here I have endeavoured to put down mostly things that would have had a devastating impact on many boys after leaving the school, and I myself noticed through the years how it affected some, including me.

I can back up these statements in any court of law. Right from the Preliminaries to the Supreme Court of law. So I have tended to leave out minor incidents, abuses, and penalties without any cause, which happened on a daily basis at St. Therese.

Brother Lepeigne was a man dedicated to preserving the image of Superiority of the Semi-Super Race of Whiteman over Indian, like the German Super Race tried to establish during the time of Hitler's regime. As I look back, what was happening at the school was basically the same thing, except on a smaller scale with the same principles.

When I got out of school in March 1944, I was already starting to feel the pangs of revenge, and I was very well trained to take punishment of all sorts. Why, if we eight- to ten-year-old kids were caught fighting as kids have done from time immemorial, and Brother Lepeigne caught us being belligerent, he would grab us by the ears, and with the other kids form a circle like a boxing ring or a wrestling ring. Then he ordered us to go for it.

"Come on now, Soweese, come on, fight! You always wanted to fight, come on, fight!"

Fight with the hollering and laughter of the watching kids. No fight was stopped until one gave up or bled too much from the nose. In the playroom we always had a punching bag strapped to the ceiling and the cement floor. That is where I learned punching at nine years old. So with all those dog fights and boxing with boxing gloves, I learned the hard way how to survive once I got out of St. Therese. I would never let another human abuse me again, and I've been fighting everything since then, from bullies to racist bastards.

This makes me think again about Brother Lepeigne, who never swayed from his ways of total domination in his position of boys' keeper. He was the complete lord and general of all fifty-five boys that were supposedly in his care, and as I think of it now, he was somehow paranoid in his position of authority and wanted to show who was boss.

I have many more stories about all that transpired between the years of 1927 and 1944, when I left school, and I have some more stories told to me after that time as well. But I sincerely hope that what I have related here will have some impact, so all that has happened in our school, and other schools in all parts of Canada—the abuse and terror in the lives of Indian children—does not occur ever again.

Let me return to one of those times when I and two of my fellow students were made to kneel on the hard, cold, cement floor for three hours after everyone went upstairs to sleep. We didn't dare to go to the washroom because Lepeigne told us to stay put and not move until he came to wake us up. Just before midnight two of us had peed our pants, and he asked us why we didn't use the toilet. We told him that he'd told us not to move. Two of us had to sleep on the cement floor of the playroom with soggy pants, and of course we got beaten with the corrugated hose the very next morning, and that went on time after time. How many times, I can't recall.

If you breached, or didn't do exactly what you were ordered to do, like whispering during silence, or if you poked someone in the ribs, you were made to write up to five hundred times with pencil and paper: *I will not poke anyone in the ribs.* Or fart, or whatever else you did that was on Lepeigne's list of "Don'ts."

It is something that is hard to forget. I can prove beyond anyone's doubt that the two wounds on my head are quite visible and can be felt by putting a finger on them. For the last sixty years or so, I still feel the pain every day.

NOW, HERE IS a memory about the end of my school days, the time I was on my way by train to Atik and on to Flin Flon, where me and my family stayed for a whole month, waiting for the snow to melt away so we could head north to our trapline. This was one of the happiest days of my life, free from pain and loneliness. It was like coming out of incarceration for a little while, that first real look at Flin Flon.

Another great thing came that same year. In the fall of 1945, my father decided that we should go up to the southern part of Reindeer Lake, a place appropriately called Deep Bay, a place that everyone in the area of Southend knew was abundant with lake and brown trout. So we all decided to build a large log cabin and a fish storage shed, and we waited for freeze-up. At that time there was an abundance of reindeer, and they used to come as far south as Sandy Bay and Flin Flon. Maybe they had fuzzy eyesight or maybe they were curious to get a whiff of us, but we would watch by our fishing nets as hundreds of reindeer crossed the lake and approached us on the shoreline, where we would shoot them. So we, the family, and our dog teams were always very well fed.

The following rough sketch gives you some idea of what I been playing with, the notion to do a pictorial history of how I lived. And I want to end with this good memory of the fishing and all the reindeer up north.

Afterword

DURING THE MONTH OF JUNE 2014, HAVING SUB-
mitted my manuscript to the University of Regina Press,
I was given the task of locating Augie so that he could
sign a contract for his memoir to be published. I knew he
was living in Prince Albert, and I had heard that he was
in poor health. But none of my contacts in Prince Albert
knew where he was living. My first of several trips yielded
a few clues. Ever since the weather turned warm, Augie
had stopped coming to the Indian Métis Friendship Centre. He had instead been seen sitting in a park near City
Hall, which at least meant that he was not in hospital.

I drove to the park in question on a warm sunny day.
I got out of my car, grabbed my book bag with contract
inside, and began to stalk the borders of the park. I wasn't

sure I would recognize Augie if I saw him. Probably not, but at least I could approach someone and ask about him.

I spotted a Métis couple, perhaps in their late seventies, chatting companionably on a park bench under the shade of a big tree. I walked up to them, hoping that I didn't look too much like a plainclothes officer or some kind of snoop.

"Sorry to intrude," I said. "Do either of you know an old fellow named Augie Merasty?"

The man looked me over for a long moment.

"Did you see that bus over there?"

I looked in the direction of the bus stop and shook my head.

"Augie was on that bus," said the man.

"You could follow that bus," said the woman.

"Where's it going?" I said.

"West," said the man.

I rushed back to my car and drove past the bus stop. I looked up and down the intersection. And the next intersection. No buses in sight. I drove back downtown to the Indian Métis Friendship Centre. One of the women told me about Buddy's, a small convenience store south and west of the downtown area. Outside the store, she said, was a dark green bench.

"He likes to sit on that bench sometimes."

She even gave me a description: "Augie wears shades

and a baseball cap, an old blue jacket, black pants and black shoes." Thus equipped, I drove to the street in question and staked it out. No one showed up to sit on the green bench.

My second trip to Prince Albert was much like the first. It was like chasing a figure in a dream, a man who dissolves before you can talk to him. People walked by the green bench outside Buddy's, and I began to think every old man I saw was Augie Merasty. It was the same in the park near City Hall.

On my third trip to Prince Albert, I spoke with a woman at the Indian Métis Friendship Centre who was filling in for the woman who usually spoke with me. She told me that I might try phoning the detox centre attached to the Victoria Hospital in Prince Albert. I brought out my cell phone.

"No," said the woman, "not now. Phone early in the morning."

Early on the morning of June 27, yawning my way toward consciousness, I dialed the detox centre and asked the woman on the phone if she knew a man named Augie Merasty. Her name was Beth.

"He's here," she said.

My heart did a back flip, and I wondered if I was dreaming.

Beth said, "He's right here. I'll put him on the phone for you."

"Hello?" I said. "Hello, Augie?"

Instead of a human voice there came the sound of music, an ethereal pulsing melody and then a soprano mouthing vowels in a tremulous voice—as though Augie's soul were being transmitted from a celestial realm.

"Hello?" I said again.

The music continued, New Age meditative warbling of some kind, and I knew I wasn't dreaming, just sleepy.

A voice uttered my name. "Davey?"

❀ ❀ ❀

AUGIE AND I agreed to meet at the detox centre a few days later. He was a frequent customer there, and slept there most nights. At his own request, he would be released routinely each morning, and then he would return at night.

I drove back up to Prince Albert to meet him on the appointed day, contract in hand, but Augie wasn't there. I explained to the young man at the desk what my plight was.

"We can't pay Augie an advance for his book until he signs the contract," I said.

"His book?" the man said. "He has a book?"

I described Augie's memoir to him and the man showed genuine interest. His name was Edmund.

"He was always talking about his book but all he had with him was this pile of papers."

The manuscript! I had sent it to him in November of 2013. But why had he never acknowledged receiving it? Why had he failed to answer my calls and letters? I asked Edmund about this.

"He's still drinking," said Edmund, as though this explained everything. "He lives on the street."

ONE NIGHT IN July I phoned the detox centre on a hunch. It was probably around midnight. I asked the man at the desk if Augie were sleeping there. It was Edmund again.

"Yes," said Edmund, "he's here right now."

"If I came up to Prince Albert real early, could you hold him for me?"

"We aren't allowed to make them stay," said Edmund, "but we'll see what we can do."

I agreed to show up very early, and once again I was given permission to enter the centre. After a few hours of sleep, I stumbled into my car and drove from Saskatoon to Prince Albert in the half-light. A dream from a few hours past came back to me. Of late, I'd been having Augie dreams. In this one, I had been searching for him in an abandoned dust-laden museum filled with stuffed animals. I would spot him in a dimly lit room and call his name, and he would dart away. Like the Greek god Proteus, he kept changing his shape from human to animal. When at last I ran him down, he was crouched in a dark corner, small as a rodent, afraid to look up at me. He began to melt like an ice carving right before my eyes. I called his name, but all that was left was a puddle of water.

I arrived around 6:30, made my way to the detox centre, and parked the car. I showed up at the door, they let me in, and I sat in a small enclosure just beyond the lobby. A few minutes later a small man trudged in, assisted by a walker. He was wearing a white hospital robe over a pair of blue pajamas. He seemed uneasy about his dishevelled appearance. He was a shrunken version of the Augie I had met a decade ago in the bar. We approached each other and shook hands.

"I'm a little hungover," he said, and sat in the chair beside me.

"I'm a little sleepy," I said.

His hair and beard were turning white and his face was so compelling to behold that I forgot to look for the scars he described in his memoir. At first, he looked as though he had stepped too soon off a merry-go-round, and yet his face kept calling back my attention. It was booze-racked and scarred, but tough, determined, and observant; his eyes gazed at me through narrow slits.

"It's good to see you at last," I said.

Augie nodded.

"I've been looking for you for a long time," I told him. "I'm glad you waited for me."

"Hmph," was all he said to that, and I wondered what kind of persuasion the detox employees had used to detain him.

"You got my book?" he said.

"Not yet, Augie. We need to sign a contract and then we'll send you some money."

"When do I get my book?"

"Not for a while, Augie."

"How long could it take to get a book out?" he said.

He was looking cranky, but perhaps he was also trying to be civil to me.

"I got the prostate cancer," he said. "I don't have a long time to live."

I asked one of the women at the desk to witness the contract. Augie signed in large, slanted, sprawling letters, the same bold cursive I had laboured over for so long. How much of the old Augie was still present, I could not tell. He was impatient, grumpy, as though everything he had to do for this damned publication was an encumbrance. Gone entirely was that devil-may-care attitude, that merry tone he used to greet me with over the phone.

Augie needed money for a cab. He wanted to go downtown. Back to the street, back to the drinking that doomed and sustained him each day. I gave him twenty bucks.

"Thanks," I said to Augie. "Thanks for waiting."

He shrugged.

Our meeting lasted perhaps twenty minutes. With contract in hand, I headed for my car. I had just opened the door when Augie came outside and called to me. He had a smile on his face.

"Hey, Davey, how d'ya like my new set a clothes?"

He was still wearing his hospital robe and pale-blue pajamas.

"Can't go downtown lookin' like this, ah?"

We both had a good laugh, and just then I realized something: the good people at the detox centre, knowing how important this meeting was for Augie and me, must have hidden Augie's clothes! Soon he would have them back. He would find his way down the hill and back to the street. He would get back to the desolate comfort of boozing, but perhaps he would be buoyed by the knowledge that his book was coming out. At that moment, Augie had reverted to the intelligent man on a quest that I had first known. He was both men, the hopeless alcoholic facing senility and the cheerful warrior and backwoods philosopher. I remembered how he had once suggested to me that his art work and his writings might allow him to last in people's memories beyond his death.

"This book of yours, Augie?"

He had turned away to go back into the detox centre, and he turned back to face me, one hand on the door.

"It's your immortality."

Augie nodded and smiled. At that moment, Augie Merasty was no longer a fleeting vision, a character that vanishes in a dream. He was right there in front of me, as big as life. Bigger than life. More than just a man. More like a hero.

Postscript

IT HAS BEEN SIXTEEN MONTHS, AS OF THIS WRIT-
ing (July 8, 2016), since Mark Medley broke the story of
this volume in the *Globe & Mail*'s "Globe Arts" section.
"The Education of Augie Merasty," he told the country,
"might be one of the most important titles to be published this spring . . . . It's a story of resilience and per-
severance—the tale of a man not only haunted by his
past, but haunted by the fundamental need to tell his
own story." Medley's major spread on March 21, 2015, was
soon followed by glowing commentary by the staff of the
National Post and by Heather Mallick of the *Toronto Star*.
Anna Maria Tremonti of CBC Radio's *The Current* said that
Augie's memoir "is so small, but it's such a mighty book."
Local journalists in Saskatchewan, from John Gormley
to Leisha Grebinski, Bill Robertson, Cam Fuller, Scott

Larson (and many more), engaged in a year-long conspiracy to cover and praise the book. It was nominated for at least six literary awards, provincial and national, and it was singled out as the inaugural title in the *One Book, One Province* initiative sponsored by the Saskatchewan Library Association to promote this title throughout 2017. With this book, Augie Merasty has become a local celebrity who is now part of a vital national conversation about racism and reconciliation. In turn, Augie has made me, for a short time, a bit more prominent than I am used to.

An old rogue, wretched father, and a drunk, suddenly redeemed. A novelist, arguably past his prime, unexpectedly sampling the limelight. Alone, we had muddled along our separate paths, but together, Augie and I witnessed an unusual ascent. If there is any gold to unearth among these unlikely prospects, it is surely to be found more in the book than in its makers. The book is the real story. My own quiet, happily obscure, writerly existence was changed overnight with awards, readings, interviews, and literary celebrations. I could be bragging here. Why deny it? I bring this news with obvious pride and gratitude. But for this new edition of *The Education of Augie Merasty* I want to report the book's success in a different tone: not pride, nor self-centered exuberance, nor even gratitude, but gladness and awe for the man who suffered so much for this story.

For all of his flaws, Augie became something of a hero
for me, a fighter for a worthy cause, a man of unusual
courage, determination, and resilience. I must confess
that I thought we would lose him before I even brought
the manuscript to a close, or before we could sign him
to a book contract, and certainly well before he could
sample the fruits of his labour. As I've already mentioned
in the Introduction to this volume, I discovered, late in
2013, that he might still be alive. When I found Augie
in Prince Albert more than a year later, I heard reports
from his daughter Arlene of his declining health: challenges with his blood pressure, his prostate cancer, his
diabetes, problems with his well-tested bladder, and his
alcoholism. Augie was eighty-five years old and still
living on the street. I could not believe that he would
make it past 2015, but Augie never seems to conform
to expectations.

He is now eighty-six years old. He is off the street
and off the booze. His daughters have corraled him and
tucked him into a seniors' residence in Prince Albert, a
place where apparently there is no boozing. In this I see
a merry bit of revenge.

I first saw the redeemed Augie at the Saskatchewan
Book Awards announcements in the Frances Morrison
Library in Saskatoon. He was alert and irrepressible.
He looked much better than he *deserved* to look. He

complained to me that Kathie Bird's inspired portrait of him (see back jacket flap) "made him look too old." Surrounded by some of Saskatchewan's most distinguished writers, Augie learned that his book had been nominated for three awards. He sprang to his feet and delivered an impromptu speech to the assembled book lovers. It ended with the words, "And if you want to find out what really happened to me in that awful place, *Buy the book!*"

With the air of a celebrity, he strode through the various departments of the library and introduced himself to the librarians. In a matter of months, Augie had become a bookseller's dream come true. He will be eager to tell you that *The Education of Augie Merasty* has now become a bestseller.

The Saskatchewan Book Awards were celebrated on April 30, 2016, at the Conexus Arts Centre in Regina. Augie was there with a dozen or more members of his extended family, including his youngest daughter Arlene, who worked very effectively as a publicist for Augie's book, and his daughter Katherine, who worked with family members to get Augie off the streets and into his current home. Augie's family has rallied around him. This book has helped them to understand what Augie went through so many years ago as a small boy, and by extension, why he was such a disaster as a father and a husband. Augie and his family now appear to be considerably more affectionate with each other than I had expected. He wears his redemption proudly.

Our tables at the awards ceremony were packed closely together. At one point, Augie was sitting in the presence of some attractive young women seeking his autograph for the book. I leaned over to him and whispered, *Augie, I forgot to warn you that once you have a book out, the women will go crazy for you!* In my own experience this has been blatantly untrue, but I'd already had a glass or two of wine.

"Well, O'Davey," said Augie, "it's too late!"

For years, I had felt an uncomfortably large gap between myself and what Augie describes as "bush Indians." In my many encounters with First Nations people, I seem to have brought my white-guy guilt with me. Augie proudly describes himself as a bush Indian because he spent so much time in the bush with his family, hunting, trapping, and fishing up north. But crossing from my table at the Conexus Centre to Augie's table, where he sat with his extended family, was like visiting my next-door neighbours. They had read the book. They had heard about our collaboration over a span of almost fourteen years. I had heard stories about the family from Augie. So we babbled away like re-united neighbours. I recall many jokes and much laughter, a great flurry of selfies, and that giddy sense of occasion, with all of us gussied up and ready to party.

This brings me to the ultimate reward of writing and re-reading Augie's story: I've discovered that it's not just a narrative about victims and victimization, not just a tale of woe in which Euro-whites attempted to force their will on Indigenous people, not just a story that highlights the differences between "us" and "them." This book is also about the things that bring people together. When you strip away the outside appearances, you are left with the common humanity of people locked in a classic struggle to save their children from the evils of coercion, abuse, and cultural extinction. Sometimes I am dogged by questions about how reconciliation might work in a permanent and meaningful way in our country, and when I do, I think about Augie's people, who are always willing and able to show me the way.

David Carpenter, Saskatoon

Study Guide

THIS STUDY GUIDE IS MEANT TO ASSIST TEACHERS in discussions about the content of this book, but it can also be used by members of book clubs or study groups, or by any other interested readers. It is hoped that by leading toward a deeper understanding of the issues that emerge in the story this guide may foster steps toward reconciliation between Indigenous and non-Indigenous peoples in Canada.

The Education of Augie Merasty provides the reader with intimate details about the experience of attending one of Canada's Indian Residential Schools as seen through the eyes of a survivor, Joseph Auguste (Augie) Merasty. Merasty's story moves the reader to a deeper understanding of Canadian history, confronts our government's policies of assimilation, and testifies to the strength of the human spirit.

It is important to deal with the history of residential schools with sensitivity. Many survivors continue to bear witness to their experiences, while others choose to keep quiet. For Indigenous students, the following discussion topics may be sensitive—especially if they have family members who are survivors of the residential school system. Others may find the topics that emerge in the book to be controversial or incomprehensible, particularly if readers feel they have no connection with the issues. In the case of some new Canadians, some of the subject matter discussed in the text may be unsettling, as it may echo some of the experiences they may have had in their former homelands. This story recounts memories of physical, emotional, spiritual, and sexual abuse.

Sensitive subject matter in the guide is indicated by the symbol ☼, providing teachers with an opportunity to prepare students for some disquieting content. Some passages in the book describe torture and sexual abuse and may not be suitable for all readers.

Introducing the Story

The Education of Augie Merasty: A Residential School Memoir captures the life of a child who attended one of Canada's government-sponsored, church-run schools located in Northern Saskatchewan. Under government-enforced policies, Indigenous children were forced to leave their homes and families and attend a boarding school intended to obliterate their cultural heritage. The schools were also intended to prepare children for their future lives in settler/colonizer society. *The Education of Augie Merasty* is the memoir of an old man about how the schooling he experienced as a boy shaped his life. His voice is courageous and, in the end, we see that a resilient spirit emerges in spite of his childhood trauma.

Background Information

INDIAN RESIDENTIAL SCHOOLS have left a dark legacy since they first opened in the nineteenth century. Saskatchewan had the last residential school in Canada: its doors finally closed in 1996. Augie Merasty was one of hundreds of thousands of Indigenous children taken from their families and forced to attend these schools. Many survivors have shared their stories of the loss of their culture, traditions, and languages. In foreign and often cruel environments, children such as Augie experienced spiritual, emotional, physical, and sexual abuse. Intergenerational trauma, a result of the residential school experience, continues to affect Indigenous families and their communities. *Multiple generations of families have experienced the damage of trauma throughout the years.*

Overarching Themes

PRIOR TO READING *The Education of Augie Merasty*, important background information should be shared and discussed. Knowledge of residential schools, the meaning of assimilation, intergenerational trauma, and the idea of reconciliation should be considered. The following themes and related questions should help guide this conversation:

Residential Schools and Indigenous People in Canada

- What were Indian residential schools and what do you know about their history in Canada?

- How and why were these schools created?

- Where in Canada did the schools operate? And during what time period?

- What religious principles did the residential schools enforce? And what were the implications in terms of the children's understanding of traditional Indigenous spirituality?

- What are the similarities and differences between contemporary "residential schools" and "Indian residential schools"?

Assimilation

- What does the term assimilation mean to you?

- Do you see evidence of assimilation today? If so, what are some examples?

- What do you think the impact of the assimilation was on Indigenous peoples, both in a historical and contemporary sense?

Intergenerational Trauma

- What is your understanding of the term "intergenerational trauma"?

- How do you think intergenerational trauma is created? What is an example of intergenerational trauma?

- What are the impacts of intergenerational trauma?

Reconciliation

- Reconciliation can have numerous meanings for different people and in varying contexts. What is your understanding of reconciliation?

- Truth is often associated with the term reconciliation. Why do you think this is?

- In 2008, the Truth and Reconciliation Commission was established in Canada. What was its role?

- Consider the following statement: Reconciliation is a process that relies on sincere investment from all Canadians, Indigenous and non-Indigenous peoples. What are your thoughts on this? Is there a role you could play in the process?

Reading the Story

THE FOLLOWING QUESTIONS and discussion points are meant to be considered while reading the book.

- What do you think of the image on the front cover? What might it symbolise?

- Think about the title of this book: *The Education of Augie Merasty.* Could it have more than one meaning?

- INTRODUCTION, PAGES IX–XVII. In "Augie and Me," David Carpenter recounts receiving the first letter from Augie Merasty requesting help in writing a book. What were Carpenter's initial thoughts about Merasty and his request?

- INTRODUCTION, PAGES XVII–XXXII. *The Education of Augie Merasty* was written by Joseph Auguste (Augie) Merasty with the help of David Carpenter, who acted as Merasty's editor. What was Carpenter's role as editor?

- PAGE 13. Merasty recalls Sister Mercy's favorite phrase: "Indians from the bush, what can you expect?" What does the phrase say about her perception of the children in the school? What is the impact on young Augie's self-image?

- PAGE 15. Discuss the significance of the following: "They never really practised what they preached, period." And on page 16, "*Oh God*, I used to think, *what hypocrisy.*" What are examples of hypocrisy?

☼ PAGES 18–21. Merasty recounts his memories as a victim of sexual abuse. Many other residential school survivors have shared similar experiences. Some people may be uncomfortable with such depictions, while others feel it is necessary for us to acknowledge that these things happened to many children. Why would some people object to these stories? Why would others feel they are necessary to tell? What is your opinion?

• PAGES 23–25. Throughout the book, Merasty revisits memories of the people who worked in the school, such as Brother Languir. "Languir was totally French," Augie remembers. "He scarcely spoke a word of English." He also recalls that Languir called another student in the school, Cyril Dorian, whose sister he was fond of, *nīstāw* ("brother-in-law" in Cree), which was the only word Languir knew in the Cree language. What is the significance of the role of limited language and communication? How did this affect young Augie's understanding and his education?

• PAGE 27–28. As an adult, Augie Merasty meets William "Scotty" Cameron in the old folks home in The Pas, Manitoba. Why do you suppose he would meet with this person? How do you think he felt after their meeting?

❂ PAGES 30–35. Merasty relives his memories of another school employee, Johannes Verwelkend, and his treatment of some of the boys, and wonders "why this man was not reported to the authorities." Discuss your thoughts and opinions of the possible reasons this employee remained at the school. What were the conditions of the time?

❂ PAGES 45–49. Merasty speaks of the physical and sexual abuse that he and other students experienced at the hands of Brother Lepeigne. Lepeigne beat and threatened young Augie, telling him to keep his "mouth shut about that sexual abuse," and Augie states, "He did a good job, because I have never told anyone about those assaults, until now." Both as a young child and later as an adult, Augie Merasty did not talk about his experiences with Brother Lepeigne. Why do you think it took him such a long time to share his experience?

❂ PAGE 50. Augie Merasty has shared his experiences of many sexual violations, and here he states, "But as things were at that time, priest, nuns, brothers belonging to the order of the Oblates of Mary Immaculate were considered by all Catholics to be infallible . . . . " What does this statement mean?

- PAGE 50. Merasty goes on to say, " . . . and they were respected with unshakeable reverence, especially by my parents…." What are your thoughts about this statement?

- PAGES 57–58. When he was in his late teens, Merasty and another former student of St. Therese ran into Brother (Brer) Lepeigne in The Pas and took him to an abandoned building. What is your reaction to what they did to Lepeigne?

- PAGES 60–62. Augie Merasty says, "All I have stated about incidents regarding our keepers at St. Therese are absolutely true . . . . " Why do you think Merasty felt the need to write his stories down? Can you think of more than one reason?

- PAGE 73. At the end of the book, David Carpenter meets Augie Merasty in Prince Albert, Saskatchewan, for the first time in a decade. Of the end of the meeting Carpenter wrote, "At that moment, Augie Merasty was no longer a fleeting vision, a character that vanishes in a dream. He was right there in front of me, as big as life. Bigger than life. More than just a man. More like a hero." Carpenter also called Merasty a hero in the introduction on page xxxvi. Why do you think Carpenter came to see Augie Merasty as a hero? Does he fit your own idea of a hero? Why?

Questions for After Reading the Book

• What do you think life was like during the time young Augie Merasty went to school in the late 1930s and early 1940s? What part of the memoir supports your answers?

• Augie Merasty briefly describes his early life before attending residential school, and then describes building a cabin and hunting and fishing with his family at the end of his school days. How do you think these settings shaped his understanding of his culture? Provide an example.

• Discuss the importance of the setting in the residential school. What were the differences between life at home and life at St. Therese? And how might these differences conflict with Augie Merasty's cultural understanding?

• What was life like for a student attending residential schools during this time? What parts of the memoir support your answers?

☼ Many children who attended residential schools have borne witness to stories of physical and sexual abuse at the hands of people who worked in the schools,

many of whom represented a specific religious domination. What belief systems were in place when residential schools operated? And how did these beliefs
affect the curriculum in residential schools?

- Other abuse was psychological. What evidence in
  Augie Merasty's story would support claims of psychological abuse? Provide examples.

- What relationships developed between young Augie
  and the staff who worked at the schools? And what
  do you think were the long-term effects of these
  relationships on Augie's life? Did they affect his relationships with people as he got older?

- Of all the people teaching or caring for the children
  at St. Therese Residential School, who do you think
  was the most admirable, and why? Who was the most
  reprehensible, and why?

- Why do you think David Carpenter agreed to work
  with Augie Merasty to help him write his memoir?

- Why do think it took such a long period of time to
  complete the memoir?

- What relationship existed between Augie Merasty
  and David Carpenter in the beginning?

- What relationship develops between Augie Merasty and David Carpenter in the end of the memoir?

- What does the term resistance mean to you? Can you find examples of resistance in Augie Merasty's memoir?

Further Discussion

- The Truth and Reconciliation Commission of Canada heard hundreds of stories from people who attended residential schools as children. Part of the Commission's work was to listen to the stories of survivors, such as Augie Merasty. Do you find his story credible? If not, explain your reasons. If so, what things make it credible for you?

- List the characteristics of the residential school system that created conditions for the abuses to occur.

- Most of what Augie Merasty recounts in his memoir takes place between 1935 and 1944. Do you think his story is relevant today?

- If you think Augie Merasty's story is relevant today, then you likely agree that residential schools have left a dark legacy for all Canadians. What do you think are some of the lasting effects on Indigenous people? What do you think are the lasting effects on non-Indigenous people?

For Teachers

THIS BOOK IS finding its way into many Canadian classrooms, and it is hoped that this study guide will further help high school teachers across Canada to introduce it to their students. This book is appropriate for courses in Indigenous Studies, Canadian History, English Language Arts, Humanities, Interdisciplinary Studies, Native Studies, Social Sciences, and Social Studies.

Acknowledgements

I WANT TO ACKNOWLEDGE THE HELP I RECEIVED from the courageous and enthusiastic people at University of Regina Press. Bruce Walsh is not only a dedicated director and publisher; he is a fighter for good, progressive, and sometimes perilous causes. David McLennan, the house editor, was a genial and wise conspirator in this unusual task we set for ourselves. I am thankful for all the advice he gave me. He was ably assisted by the U of R Press's managing editor, Donna Grant. Many thanks to Edmund, Marla, Martha, Beth, Lorna, and their co-workers at the detox centre in Prince Albert, who welcomed me at their workplace and helped me run Augie down; and to Sharon, Tina, and their colleagues at the Indian Métis Friendship Centre of Prince Albert for some helpful liaison and detective work. Thanks to Brian Walmark from the Northern Chiefs Council of Keewaytinook Okimakanak for advice on how to approach publishing this manuscript, and thanks to Helen Yum for providing legal advice. Thanks to James (Sa'ke'j) Young-blood Henderson, Joseph Naytowhow, and Jim Miller for some historical background on residential schools. Thanks to Sarah Longman with Regina Public Schools for her work preparing the study guide for this new edition. And a big thank you to Augie's daughter, Arlene Merasty, for her support. *kinanāskomitin.*

David Carpenter
Winter, 2016

ABOUT DAVID CARPENTER

Born and raised in Edmonton, David Carpenter first began writing as a translator in Edmonton and Winnipeg. Before becoming a full-time writer he was a professor at the University of Saskatchewan, and during this time he taught English classes to aboriginal students in Prince Albert. His first novel, *Banjo Lessons,* won the City of Edmonton Book Prize (1998). His collection of novellas entitled *Welcome to Canada* (2009) won Foreword Review's silver medal for short fiction (Michigan) and the Independent Booksellers' Association gold medal for Western Canadian Fiction (New York) in 2010. In the following year, his memoir, *A Hunter's Confession,* was awarded Saskatchewan's Book of the Year. He is married to the artist Honor Kever.

THE REGINA COLLECTION

Named as a tribute to Saskatchewan's capital city with its rich history of boundary-defying innovation, The Regina Collection builds upon University of Regina Press's motto of "a voice for many peoples." Intimate in size and beautifully packaged, these books aim to tell the stories of those who have been caught up in social and political circumstances beyond their control.

OTHER BOOKS IN *The Regina Collection:*

Time Will Say Nothing:
A Philosopher Survives an Iranian Prison
by Ramin Jahanbegloo (2014)

The Education of Augie Merasty:
A Residential School Memoir
by Joseph Auguste Merasty,
with David Carpenter (2015)

Inside the Mental:
Silence, Stigma, Psychiatry, and LSD
by Kay Parley (2016)

Otto & Daria:
A Wartime Journey through No Man's Land
by Eric Koch (2016)

Towards a Prairie Atonement
by Trevor Herriot (2016)

THE REGINA COLLECTION

N AMED AS A tribute to Saskatchewan's capital city with its rich history of boundary-defying innovation, The Regina Collection builds upon University of Regina Press's motto of "a voice for many peoples." Intimate in size and beautifully packaged, these books aim to tell the stories of those who have been caught up in social and political circumstances beyond their control.

OTHER BOOKS IN *The Regina Collection:*

Time Will Say Nothing:
A Philosopher Survives an Iranian Prison
by Ramin Jahanbegloo (2014)

The Education of Augie Merasty:
A Residential School Memoir
by Joseph Auguste Merasty,
with David Carpenter (2015)

Inside the Mental:
Silence, Stigma, Psychiatry, and LSD
by Kay Parley (2016)

Otto & Daria:
A Wartime Journey through No Man's Land
by Eric Koch (2016)

Towards a Prairie Atonement
by Trevor Herriot (2016)

ABOUT DAVID CARPENTER

Born and raised in Edmonton, David Carpenter first began writing as a translator in Edmonton and Winnipeg. Before becoming a full-time writer he was a professor at the University of Saskatchewan, and during this time he taught English classes to aboriginal students in Prince Albert. His first novel, *Banjo Lessons*, won the City of Edmonton Book Prize (1998). His collection of novellas entitled *Welcome to Canada* (2009) won Foreword Review's silver medal for short fiction (Michigan) and the Independent Booksellers' Association gold medal for Western Canadian Fiction (New York) in 2010. In the following year, his memoir, *A Hunter's Confession*, was awarded Saskatchewan's Book of the Year. He is married to the artist Honor Kever.